A PRODIGAL

MAN

From a young youth of trails into the cycle's of a prison

Wall.

My story of transformation and amends.

By

DERRICK ROBINSON

ISBN:
Paperback: 978-1-971141-19-0
Hardcover: 978-1-971141-20-6

Published by: Columbus Book Publishers

www.columbusbookpublishers.com/

Printed in the United States of America

Dedication

In the world through which I travel, I am endlessly creating myself.

Frantz Fanon.

Acknowledgments

With much gratitude and love to Jamie Hurston, and to the courageous brothers, who accepted me as I was and inspired me with the knowledge and values that helped me understand my world.

I give fervent praise to God, who gave me new meaning and a purpose in life.

To James Robinson, I miss you, your nourishment, love, and guidance still inspires. Forever, R.I.P.

To the Prison Riot Radio our support, reporter, and journalist Jay – I thank you always for your courage, trust, and strength and the actions you took and sacrifices you made on our behalf.

To Ethel Hurston, Sharon, Sandra, Ronald, Asia and the Hurston family for your support and love.

To my comrade, mentor, and brother Fredrick for all you have done more than 15 years of struggle and loyalty.

And to my mother Ethel Robinson most of all. I want to thank you for giving me life and the lessons that have endured me along the way. You are truly loved always.

About the Author

Derrick Robinson is currently serving a prison term 9 Life sentences, and 30 years consecutive (Armed robbery, Kidnapping, and firearm) convictions in a single Subway restaurant in Douglasville Georgia on October 1,1999. Along with his first storytelling book A Prodigal Man Derrick Robinson plans to further his work, and invite you towards such changes in his journey. His work has been adapted for strength and determination. At 54 years he has survived the state of Georgia and the Department of Corrections.

YouTube: *Prison Riot Radio, Derrick Robinson (Over sentence case and Living art).*

Prologue

The prison world is just a small mirror of the real society. For each season a man is measured upon the life he chooses. And throughout the two decades living behind a prison wall. I've experience many changes. Some mental, spiritual, and physical. I've met them all.

The reality of it is Doing the time. Not the time doing you. And knowing who you are is over rated in prison. Like being Latino, Muslim, Christian, or Blood. All have their place in our community. But I notice, on a larger scale. Is that these brothers want to forever remain young. And that's not possible no matter what choice you made in life. Life has it's own set of rules.

Just because you fail the test. Don't mean you can't still progress later in life. I've met some O.Gs throughout my bid. Who have made changes for the better. Around that time I was living a religious lifestyle here in prison. I was stunned at a clergyman words who said, There are no real religious people in prison. That's a lie. Now he may have meant there are some people that deserve to be in prison. But that's not his call. It's not his decision to set the guidelines for such people.

Rather, it's the GDC of pardons who decides those matters. But I do believe it's a person's responsibility to make a strong effort towards redefining themselves. In a positive way prior to their release. To realize life goodness. Brothers must know and accept it's course and create their life's within it. In my understanding how this cycle works. A long standing, I recall some very difficult moments coping. And just when things began to make sense. I was setting in a jail awaiting trail for a twenty count indictment. I was begging for forgiveness, feeling remorse for every soul I have ever wronged. Still today. I remember the judge words as I looked him in the eyes. Son, I have never handled a case where the robber had took, not just the store money.

But also the money from the customers. You facing a very long time in prison. That was the birth of my transformation, a point where my reality got serious. Like there are two sides to a coin. I just knew that was my calling. So beginning my search for the truth. I searched high and low about my situation trying to puzzle the pieces together. I was surprised when I discovered that my later life. Is just a reflection of my earlier life.

So growing up has to do with getting rid of the extra baggage and the like. Acting foolish is the opposite. Identifying your true self is work. Like anything in life, we must want it before the progress or changes begin. A Prodigal Man isn't about a prison experience. It's a literary that shows how the prison world made an impact on my life. And also how I used the time mostly on the Tier Program at Valdosta State Prison.

To view life differently, making such changes to better understand the man I am today. In addition, I know these brothers have families and friends beyond these walls. They may not be aware what their love one is going through here in prison.

Table of Contents

PART I

CHAPTER 1

I lived a very normal life since the beginning. So it seemed when I was five. I learned the difference between my family. My oldest sister Michelle and my youngest sister Lashanda. People always use to say Shan and I could pass as twins, the way we bonded together. Growing up we were in some ways inseparable. I always thought it was because we both inherited the same father blood line. If my sister was to die today. I'm not sure how I would take the lost here in prison. A lot has changed since our childhood days. We aren't as close as we were then. Our mother always taught us the golden rule. Treat each other with kindness now. Because when it's said and done, tomorrow you will regret what you did wrong.

If I go back I guess that's when my pain all begins. No I didn't listen to my mother. I've let down so many people. That's the hard part of coping with prison life, and most everyone I knew then. Are no longer part of my life now. Another reason that inspired me to write this story. It gives me a sense of purpose, a real meaning to keep moving forward. So you know this story isn't for show off. It's just my truth. I was what you call a hard head boy. Very quick to anger and a little emotional at times. I was into landscaping yards by the time I was ten years old. The best man I ever knew was my father. Yes. I said my father, kind of strange word for most people but I prefer calling him my dad. The second best man was my uncle Jimmy. Those two men taught me about responsibility and life. Dad also taught me about parenting, and learning skills with my hands. Although I became better at arts and crafting wood, skills I acquired on my own.

My dad James died from contracting diabetes in 2013. I really miss the most influential man in my life time. Although both men inspired me I still live out their legacy after loosing them here in prison. May their soul rest in peace. Fortunately as time past. I had another childhood role model my friend Malcolm. He was the most prodigal child I ever met. I learned to shoplift, and steal cars, at the age thirteen. I simply told him. Man I want to do what you do. I'm tired of being broke. Malcolm told me to meet him one day after school. And make sure you bring a book bag he, said. As our friendship grew I learned more about him. He was taught by his older brother who was at the time a major drug dealer. It was discovered in 2009, that Malcolm was murdered while sitting in his car. I heard rumors that it was a drug deal gone bad, while others say he had a contract on his life. Between, the both of them I'd acquired a level of criminal activities hustling in the streets. I stole expensive BMWs, Porches, and Mercedes Benz. I sold drugs for fun because I didn't like the long hours it took just to make a sale. So I extended the car theft business into opening a chop shop. Then at the age sixteen I learned the robbing game. A mishaps I'll never forget but regret the moment I bout my first semi automatic. You named the spot. I took it from anybody hustling drugs on the streets. I was robbing a city on every block before I was twenty- one. All the while I was creating a bad image and building a criminal record. I look back at those earlier stages in my life, wishing I could press rewind. But that's impossible to do. Life isn't a game.

I'll be lying to tell you I grew up well off. Even though my parents back in the 80s were considered to be a younger couple. They were destined to be kids first but never had a chance it seems to have real fun. Not like these parents are about now. Mrs. Ethel Robinson carried the responsibility of being a house wife. While, her husband duty was juggling a 9 to 5 out side the house hold. Together, they both insured the basic needs their three children depended on to sustain life. I went to a public school at Boulder View Elementary East Atlanta. This is where I adopted the name Tar baby. You might say I was gullible, fat, or riding the little yellow tinted window bus to school. But, that's hardly the case, simply put l definitely was the opposite. I was just strange in my own way. I still hold the view that school isn't where real leaning happens in my opinion. I picked up skills mostly outside those classrooms, both beneficial and non beneficial knowledge. While the school of hard knocks appeared more real living under pressure in such poor conditions. I'll never get to old forgetting my roots. But it's important to know that such institutions is needed for the purpose of higher learning. Like Warren's Boys

Club homage to my boxing mentor Evander Holyfield. Where I learned a combination followed by a upper cut took care a fight. Then there was a summer program U-Can my parents sent me to. I guess their intention was to ensure security. Things like personal growth and accountability. Now that I think about it, everything make sense because the moment I arrive home. I was completely exhausted mentally.

My parents had to know the signs. Because boys are more active, more demanding of attention than girls I believe. And for some reason like to do things we shouldn't be doing. So my mother was quick to give me a whipping. Which was different from the beatings I received from my father. The whole idea spoiled me rotten for carrying out punishment. It, simply didn't work for me. The more I talk to you. The more hard head you get, mama said. I don't know where the idea U-Can came about. Just maybe some friends of my parents, having the same issues with their son. But I actually liked it. And besides the dress code was cool. We only wore brown khakis with a white rugby shirt along with black sneakers. As long as I didn't have to wear my school clothes. In so many ways. I felt like a real brother to most of the boys at U- Can. In a sense having a brother around all the time at home. Being the only male at home with three females can get real ugly. My mama did what she could do while Dad was away at work.

After school I would rush home stay long enough just to drop off my book bag. Snatch some Chip Ahoy's from the kitchen. And make a b-line out the front door. Escaping the house before my mama got back home was easy. The hardest part was trying to explain why I'm failing in almost every class. Or why I'm not in my room doing homework. Instead, I was standing at the front door wearing new clothes, looking all dirty and sweaty. Felling very guilty. Mama would have a hand on her hip and the other firmly gripping a thick tree branch. Looking like a Goddess warrior ready for battle. Shut up boy! And when your Daddy get home you getting another ass whipping too.

CHAPTER 2

That would always be the case. Wasn't one ass whipping enough? I mean mama laid down some really nice swings with that switch. She knew how to use it, but she could never make me cry. Which, I figured was the reason why I was being punished twice for the same thing. So it didn't take long for me to come up with an idea. Because, my dad was the man carrying out pain. I promise myself it would end sooner. The next time I got into trouble. My mother will be sure. I'd learn my lesson. That day came sooner than I'd expected on a warm summer day. Although, the events that lead up to this incident wasn't my idea of getting a lesser punishment. I recall playing in my neighbor's yard. Cedric was my close friend. We were pretty tight attended the same school, age, grade, classmates etc. But, I secretly envied him because I never known him to get punished for leaving the house after school. So, on that day we played a game of Dare. I dared Cedric to climb this tall pine tree, seeing if he could reach the top before me. Standing a few inches taller I had the advantage over him. And it didn't take long to win. So his shame took on another game of Dare. He owned a very huge menace looking Saint Barnard. The dog, if that's what it was would bark and chase after any moving objects along the yard fence. No one in the neighborhood would dare cross its path. So now, Cedric was daring me to enter the back yard, leading up to this dog house where this monster was waiting. Don't tell me your scared he said. No, I am not scared. Then c'mon let's go and see. Bear isn't going to hurt you he said leading the way.

I must have hesitated for a minute thinking about the risk. But I had to proof to my friend I definitely wasn't a coward. Cedric couldn't have notice how I was truly feeling inside. Because he looked back at me in mock surprise when we entered the fence. What happened next seemed like a dream. All I know is that I woke up confined to my room in severe pain, stretched out on the bed. I traced the pain at my left leg seeing first aid bandage wrapped around it. Nothing but ashamed washed over me. Not because I miss calculated the five foot wall which caused me to take a nasty fall. I was embarrassed because I again disappointed my mother. She was about to have a nervous breakdown it seemed. I swore to God the next time I saw Cedric's dog. I'm going to kill it. When I recovered from the incident leaving me scared. I thought about the whole episode. You know when your mind says I wish I should've... But that's not how it happened. Unfortunately, I still got punished for being hard head for a whole month. No t.v, no outside, no allowance. No nothing. All because I didn't listen to my mother. She always reminded me that a hard head makes a soft ass. After, years of living on Boulder View. My parents moved the family to a more up scale middle class community. This was during an era, where legendary song artist Gladys Night lived in our neighborhood. The community also defined the status of modern black families. The Robinson's left behind the poor conditions and moved up the latter towards success. In the late 80s our family joined the integrated East Atlanta. The so call amenities of the new city. Emerald Estates was a district located about 10 minutes east of the city. I-20 East exit on Westley Chapel Rd. Simply, take a left crossing the bridge at the light. Then another left at the next intersection hooking a right on Rainbow Dr. Our new home set on Tiffany Cir. A spacious split level brick style, four bedroom, and very huge back yard. It even had a 10ft. basketball goal. The only thing missing was a swimming pool, but the community club house was all I needed. So during the summer times. I spent hours enjoying the Olympic size swimming pool.

Between the age 10-13. Were some of the best memories of my youth. Growing up with my family was more enjoyable than attending public schools. Similar, but not the same only better. I'm serious I hated school. Not like most kids just to please their parents. I didn't hold back my resentment. In fourth grade I met JoJo. He lived in my neighborhood plus attended my school. Oh, yeah we were also classmates in social studies. It was him who gave me the name Tar Baby. He was a class clown. And no one was exempt from his taunting no matter who you was. Tar baby you so black. I can see your reflection in the dark. Hey Tar baby. I never seen a ten year old wearing diapers. I mean the boy was a bully saying things that would really get under my skin. I'd get so mad. Sometimes I just would break down and cry, like a big baby. But, fortunately I built the courage one day shocking even myself when I yelled at him. We going to see fat boy. While I was getting a education. I also had to fight the bully's off after school. It got me through some rough times, thanks for the boxing lessons at Warren Boys Club. I was never a trouble maker. And I definitely didn't see any other option but to shut this bully up for good. Everybody had a click of friends to hang out with during school. Dwayne, Carlos, Antwan and myself were inseparable even outside of school. They had gotten the news before classes ended. News travel fast. They all asked me Are you really going to fight JoJo. Like I was not in my right mind. I just gave them a nod, like it was nothing. There was no turning back for sure. So I ignored the doubts going through my mind. And as we got closer to the meet up spot. I swear I wanted to run like hell. From here the rest gets interesting as JoJo and I paired off.

The object of boxing. Is to keep moving at all times, keeping your opponent at arms length and throwing jabs at the target. Following a swift punch with the other arm while leaning your weight into the target. Before, I realized what I done. The fight was over and JoJo never bothered me again, matter fact we became friends. Then imagine your seventh grade teacher being your neighbor as well. Ms. Brown lived two houses from me. She was the most hated teacher at school and very strict. She made it her business keeping a tight leach

10

on me every chance she got during class. Even, if it was a rumor about me misbehaving or failing in another class she was going to tell my mama. So, tell me how my mama found out about the fight after school. Now my own flesh and blood that's different. Shan acted the same way whenever I done something wrong. She frowned at me. In her little sister kind of way saying it isn't right for me throwing rocks at Mrs. Brown's dog. Then she need to stop calling Mama at home snitching on me. Well she may have been right about that but I didn't care. I'm not sure if there was a heaven for me back then. Or just maybe I was to young to know the meaning of forgiveness.

I recall things that happened long time ago that still gets me upset. Not to the point of being revengeful but the fact it happened to me or someone else. I'm working on it but it sure is hard to change the way I feel sometimes.

CHAPTER 3

Georgia will always be home. Fulton County was my birth place. It's where my parents first met, married, and raised a family together. It was a shock to learn much later on that this couple discovered each other while my dad was in jail. Dad was a huge skilled man standing at 6'5 and weighing 365lb. On account of his job under the scorching sun he was very dark skin. His salary alone was enough to ensure that the family had sufficient food to eat. James worked at Zares as a mechanic repairing eighteen wheelers. Mama always called him James, even in front of us kids. Which was a bit to formal if you ask me. I guess because back in the days black adults were called by their first names. Especially, here in the dirty south. Some black families still uphold their roots. Like the old slave trade system. A chattel slave was a worker that could be transferred or sold away from the property. And in turn the owner of a chattel slave claimed possession of his or her self. Still today, I'm at a lost about my family roots. I didn't ask those types of questions as a child growing up. And I don't remember any such lessons being taught in a text book during school. Mama, who was from a very small town called Shady Dale. I guess she was a country girl and was proud of it too. She is the most wonderful person I've ever known. Between my parents. I always favored my mama.

What we use to call a Mama's boy. Shan was the very opposite. Well I guess Michelle and Mama had a tighter bond since she never knew her real dad. Although the oldest, she pretty much stayed out the way. Her honorary in school prove to be what any parent want to expect from their child. Yeah and I envied her for being smart. She also graduated from high school along with getting married shortly afterwards.

Before Ethel married James her maiden name was Freeman. Her mother like wise gave birth to one boy and three girls. My uncle Grady, aunt Helen, and Gloria. My mother is the only child living today. My parents were always improving themselves bringing us up just the same but only better. People would look at the Robinson's and wonder where in the world this black family come from. Because like I mentioned Emerald Estates wasn't completely integrated back then. We weren't the most noble bunch, by no means. As children we were aware that we lived beyond normal but never gave it much attention. Because we were to busy enjoying being kids. It was never a dull moment I recall. Just living a young youth full of energy and love among us. Life was good. Besides being involved in basic learning skills like U-Can provided outside of home. My parents also sought the need in making sure I stayed active in sports. I join the minor league baseball team at Minor Park at ten years old. What league a boy played was determined by his age. My team was the Tigers. Antwan was in the peewee league, while Carlos and David played in the major league. After, practice we would all gather and make fun of Antwan because they didn't have pitchers in peewee league. There we were laughing our self to death. If you never seen 5-9 year old kids trying to hit a baseball setting erect on a tee. You missing out. I thought the Bad news Bears was funny. That same season my team came in second place loosing against Gresham Park. I played first base and left field most games. But every now and then coach needed me to pitch games. Being a pitcher means being up under pressure when the crowd is loud chatting. You can't hit it. You no good. Cause you come from Hollywood. And as soon as the ball leaves my hand. The guy at the home plate takes a swing and miss. Then the umpire screams strike three. There I was having the fun of my life.

But, like the saying there is two sides to a coin. Any chance beating the odds in life depends on our choices. It was during this time when the coin didn't fall in favor for the Robinson's. I notice my parents having marriage problems. One fight after the next. I saw with my own eyes and it hurt me more than anything to see them like that. Mom and Dad don't treat each other the way they do. Life is a strange thing sometimes. Just when you think you're going one way, then all of a sudden everything changes. I didn't have to ask Mama why she stayed mad all the time. I was a smart child hardly anything got pass me. I was always paying attention.

In, 1989 my mama decided it was time to leave her husband. She obviously was tired of fighting for something she felt wasn't worth holding on to. I blamed them both. But it took some time to calm myself over the big disappointment. Nothing I could do to repair my parents break up. However the memories will always be with me. It really effected the way my life turned out later. All I ever wanted was for us to stay together. One big happy family like it was at the beginning. I'll never forget coming home from school seeing a police car parked in our drive way and the signs were definitely there. I figured Mama had called the cops, just in case Dad wanted to cause trouble that day. The cops stood in our living room with Dad while we packed what little we could and loaded it in the car. I was so mad with mix emotions running through me. The things Dad did to our family was the lowest ever. He'd been a drinker for as long as I could remember but that wasn't the problem. Even, the marijuana use but never in a million years had I thought he was a cocaine addict. My dad on crack! We'll come today think of it the signs were definitely there staying out all night. Missing for 2-3 days and the constant fights with mama. So that was the straw, he really did it. Oh, yeah and the news I heard from my mama talking to my aunt on the phone. Not only did his pockets get empty but also the bank joint account. Not a penny. A sure sign his drug abuse had gotten unmanageable, in which had destroyed our family.

CHAPTER 4

Even then I knew the drugs Malcolm brother had schooled me on was the hard stuff. So I should've known at the time. Dad would get high on marijuana behind the door of their bedroom. But this new smell on a few visits had to be something else. How did I not know this? The marijuana wasn't the reason behind his drug abuse or domestic problems. Everybody knows smoking Mary Jane don't break up happy homes. And probably the reason why my parents started fighting, the moment he got hooked on dope. No one can tell me the side effects from using cocaine. It will cause anger issues, moods, or living a life of crime. Some changes in life a child can't accept, or admit without felling the pain. But that was a long time ago. Over the years learning how to recover came easy. I had to realize it was better to forgive than to remain upset. I mean things could've been a whole lot worse. And I know it was wrong blaming him but I did. Sometimes I wish the both of them could've sought professional help, rehab, marriage counseling or something. Before getting a divorce. But that's not the way it happened.

I'll always have an intense love for my parents. No matter what. Most times it seems like I didn't appreciate them being so hard headed. Honesty and respect were valued in the Robinson's home. At thirteen, I didn't know how to cope with the absence of loosing a father figure. There was no such thing as an atheist in my family. I'll always have a strong belief in God. But I never took my spirituality serious until I came to prison. As a child mama was strict when it came to the Bible. She made sure that the King James was read and memorized. I can recite 23 Psalms and Mathews 6. I was baptized at Baylor Baptist Church where we attended morning service and Sunday school. While I was grieving and feeling sorry for my lost. I was also loosing faith. Sometimes the feeling of being alone having no purpose. And not really understanding my situation caused me to bottle everything up inside. No God that loves me could take away a father like him. And I could sense the same feelings from my sister Shan. Michelle didn't seem to upset. But I'm pretty sure she loved her step Father because he was the only dad she knew. Mama suffered the most although she tried not to show it. And, still to this day. I don't think she has fully recovered from loosing her husband.

After packing up what little we could. We all moved in with aunt Gloria. She lived on the East side between Glenwood Rd. and Second Ave. The neighborhood wasn't that bad. A little on the hood side in some parts but livable all together. We stayed about three blocks from Eastlake Meadows projects. Put it this way. When you have to use a milk crate nailed to a tree, in order to play basketball. You know it's the hood. Upon getting a feel for the new place. I met new friends. Kevin lived in the back of us. He was in the dope game. Doug was too. Between the two Kevin had reached a higher position moving weight throughout the city. It was rumored about five years ago that the brothers had a beef. Doug supposedly stole some money from Kevin leaving him dead. The net worth about $75,000. Due to an informant to the where about of Doug's location. And he was later arrested. He is now serving Fed time in prison.

Just so happen I ran into JoJo in 2009. We were at Hancock State Prison in the same dorm. He plead guilty to a life sentence. Damn who did you kill? I asked, him. I guess he thought I was joking because he ignored me and kept on walking. But he looked over his shoulder as if someone was ear hustling. Remember, that nigga Doug on the East side, he was getting to the money back then. Oh, yeah I remember him. It wasn't no huge surprise to me every thug wanted a peace of the action. Even me but I couldn't take from a friend no matter how much he was worth. But I did feel like justice was settled by hearing this news because Kevin was my nigga, him and I were tight. I'll never forget the times he loan me money for making bail in the county jail. Kevin kind of put me in the mind of Malcolm. They say we all have a twin in the world. My twin was dad. I never had a role model after my parents separated someone to look up to. For the simple fact, I had a hard time trusting my homeboys in the streets. They wouldn't think twice about betraying their own blood so why should I trust them. So from that point own I kept my walls up. I mostly stayed to myself, I mean the streets have a way of bridging the gap between yourself and others.

And no matter how hard mama would try. She failed at trying to keep me out the streets and stay in school. Her preaching didn't work period. If I was a knuckle head boy years ago. I definitely wasn't in my right mind now. There was nothing Mama could do to guide me in the right direction without a father. She was convinced I guess when I dropped out of school. The streets continued to be my favorite pass time taking control of my life. Before, quitting school in the 11th grade at McNair. I enrolled in several other schools, only to get expelled for violating a rule, cutting class was a routine. However, I did enjoy playing sports at school. Wrestling and baseball. I can't believe I weighed only 105 lb. BJ was my match partner during wrestling practice. Because of his experience being a division champ in his weight class. I knew I could take down any opponent if I trained hard with BJ. I learned all types of moves from him. My favorite movie was the banana split.

On October 31,1986 Halloween night I drove along with my mother. She had a 76 Camaro she brought from her sister. We were headed to Kroger's. The one on Candler Rd. across from South DeKalb mall. When we entered the store. I decided to go in the opposite direction. A routine I had picked up. So while I'm looking around, spotting a few items to steal and making sure I'm alone. I suddenly felt some eyes on me as I quickly tucked away a item underneath my shirt. A man wearing a white apron was just standing in the distance looking at me. You know that guilt feeling! I felt it. Do you mind stepping in my office and committing, he said.

Minutes later the police arrived and I was put inside his car. I was going to jail. This was the first time ever getting locked up for committing a crime. A thousand things was eating at me. Like how can I get myself out of this jam? And why my mama didn't come to my aid before we left the store? Where is she now? But it didn't take long to realize mama absence was a statement. Her way of punishing me. I was charged for shoplifting as a juvenile it was scary as hell. She finally came to my rescue the following week. Both embarrass and upset Mama had made her point.

CHAPTER 5

Just imagine leaving behind everybody you know. And being script of everything you own. Then be given clothes you wear every day of the week. Caged up in a 6x9 cell with a toilet and sink. Next picture not having enough food to satisfy your hunger while trying to sleep overnight, knowing your breakfast want be served until another six hours. They give you a razor thin mat to sleep on. While you trying to figure your next move out, people watching, plotting and sizing you up. But all you can think about is. Why I'm here and how I'm going to get out. Collect calls are a waist of time because nobody is accepting your calls. You have to constantly be on guard 24-7. You can't show any signs of being scared or weak because you may have to fight any given moment. You have no friends. You have no privacy You pray on your bunk at night, while you cry alone. This was my repetitive cycle more times than I can remember guilty or innocent. This is how I was treated and some guards viewed me less than a human. See, this is how it works. First you get arrested which is the worst. It's the hardest to cope with because you don't know the rules. Your girl want come to visit, because when out of sight. You out of her mind. Your life and what little you own becomes state property. But if you have enough money, you can get out. You just pay 10% and bond out of jail. However, let's assume you are broke. Which means you can afford a lawyer. So the judge gives you a public defender who just wants to admit guilty.

She or He can work a deal with the D.A. Let's say you got a robbery charge and you plead guilty to 20 years. You will be on parole after serving 10 years in prison. While you was in prison you lost your home, job, girlfriend etc. You need basic living supplies to maintain so you need money. If you don't get a job you go back to prison. And you definitely don't want that to happen. Keep in mind you must have a suitable home and stable job on parole. But you are a felon, which means most jobs want hire ex-cons. So you ask yourself, What do I do now? As bad as you don't want to you start hanging out with your friends. They sale you a gun. You rob a store but then you got to keep it up to have some money. The more money you make the more deep in the hustle you get. And can not get out of the life style. That pretty much sums up my repetitive past. And it's damn shame it took all these years in prison to realize my mistakes. If I knew what I know now. I wouldn't be here in prison writing this book. But, I believe things happen for a reason as you live out any experience. I mean it's a really bad place, prison is not living a health life. And hey, don't let anyone tell you differently.

I spent a whole week in jail. The jail was supposed to change the way my life was going. Stop stealing, skipping class, and using drugs. Honesty, there was no other alternative I believed than the same choices I been making. The same old song. So, I went for what I know, self destruction. Yeah, I was to far gone to see another dead end. But I also didn't feel there was another route I could choose. For awhile mama was receiving government assistance and working part-time. Michelle manage to help out working full time towards getting her high school diploma. Gloria seemed to like the idea of having more income coming in but deep down inside she missed her privacy also. I guess we did okay. Shan and handled most of the chores around the house, since we weren't old enough to get a job. Although, I was barley attending school. Mama, never held back her demands on getting a education, thanks to Michelle's honorable passing grades. Like I said, sports was my only interest at the time, I could care less about school. All the peer pressure between those activities wasn't helping me at all. I still didn't understand why these things couldn't merge and make my life better. I was more confused than I ever been before. Like when a child comes home from school. You can bet food is the first thing on their mind. They want some new clothes just so they can show off the next day. Or better yet own their own car like the others at school.

Sometimes I would come home late from school. Lithonia High School wasn't in Atlanta. It took approximately an hour to travel there and back each day. I relied on a bus program called M to M. The Atlanta Public Schools of transportation established a transit system for mainly kids who went to schools outside their district zones. Which only increased my dislike. After wrestling practice I would ride the M to M bus to get home. It also, applied to kids that needed transportation after school. But sometimes depending on what time practice ended. I'd have to catch the public transit Marta bus. The route from Lithonia, I-20 west exiting off Capital Ave. downtown, form there I'd get on the 7 McAfee. Then take I-20 east exit off Glenwood making a right on Terry Mill. From there I'd get off on Stanton Rd. and walk two blocks up the street to my aunt's house.

... ...

In and out of trouble became a routine. A major flaws in my life. Pulling me deeper into oblivion. When I went to jail a third time. I met Albert my cell mate at Y.D.C. He was a born again Christian. And fortunately, we got alone just fine despite our differences in lifestyle. Much to my surprise he was also a car thief. We enjoyed sharing our stories about the streets how our patterns were similar, he was good. But I didn't understand why he chose living a Prodigal lifestyle oppose to being religious. And I didn't ask, either. I was to busy having fun. But, I did learn that he stole cars to support his drug addiction, the same drug that destroyed my family. One day he ask me the strangest thing. How can you not find time for God? Think of the life he gave you, the air you breathe and all the things he's given you. I thought about it long, and said. I don't know. We'll they have church tomorrow let's join fellowship together. Man I am not no Christian! I told him. Albert laughed and said, Naw bro, the service is open to everyone. So, I took up his invitation due to the fact we were friends, so far. And besides I didn't want to disappoint him. To my surprise it happened more than once, and got baptized. I attended all the services offered and enjoyed being among them brothers.

Because we all shared something alike.

CHAPTER 6

During my time in Y.D.C. I got into fights a few times and was sent to lock up. I even had some attempts of suicide using a home made knife. Cutting myself to escape the pain and anger. Another way of expressing my discomfort was throwing urine at the guards. They made checks while I was being housed in segregation. I recall my exbunkmate Albert. How he used his time constructively. He mostly read books. He simply relied on faith as a remedy for any coping issues he was going through. His favorite quote. It's not seeing but about believing no matter what happens in life. Instead, here I stood blaming God, family, and everyone else more importantly my father. The thought of being alone with a false identity of who I am. Along with a hate for others. But, still without a justifiable reason I was behaving this way. For reasons I'd learn much later that being angry was a weakness. My behavior was destroying me, delaying any hopes of making amends and restoring my life.

It's natural to get upset. Yeah, it is to the point we loose it. But it becomes unhealthy when it can't be controlled. I was in so much pain. Deep down inside mama was counting on me to help our dis-

functional family. Let her tell it. Her son was the heir of the James she lost. Which only gave me even more excuses to hustle the streets.

If Dad could do it then I could too. And just having that taste for that life I chose for myself. At times like this made me wish things were different, maybe I should've listen to mama.

In my sophomore year at McNair. I dropped out of school. Not because of failing in all my classes. Believe it or not I was making average passing grades, just a summer at night school to earn a little more SAT points. And I could've furthered my education. I even tried getting my GED but that didn't work either. I just couldn't stay long enough to finish. So it wasn't no use trying, so I gave up. Michelle had graduated that same year. She was dating her high school sweetheart. She agreed to sale me her Toyota for $300. I figured it was a fair deal since it needed some new parts. Mama and Gloria was so proud of her finishing grade school. She was making a few advances and plans of getting married soon. I had always envied her because of that alone. Especially, the way mama was always comparing us. If she can finish school then so can you. Y'all aren't no different. We were all one and the same person in mama eyes. But that's not the way I seen it. Like the saying. All men are created equal, which implies that all men would do each task equally also. Everybody would be able to jump as high or run as fast. There wouldn't be no basis for winning a goal medal. Now would it? Let's ask ourselves. What made me this way? Why is he a drug dealer? Do you think he was born that way? Or, he woke up and said, I want to be a jail bird!

Well at the time. It was obvious why my life was treading down the wrong road. Yeah a choice I made. It was decided by my parents to raise me up to become a good child. To show me how to be a better boy and hope that some day. Later in life. The lessons would help me to become a better man. To sum it up. Those plans wasn't the life their son took for granted. Michelle did though. She made the grades, honorary, married, and manage to raise two kids. Her daughter followed her footsteps living a similar experience. I'll admit they did well. Some how we ended up going in different directions growing up. How did she do it? I guess she already had her life planned while me and Shan was still figuring life out. However, we all grew up with Mama under poor conditions and Michelle didn't turn out like me.

... ...

I want to talk a little about sex. I guess parents in the 80s didn't know how to talk to their children about sexuality. Both homosexual and hero sexual. Which was the case in the Robinson's home. My parents took the silent role on this subject, something that makes me wonder if things would've been different. As far as I can remember. There was never a time I witness the acts being taught inside our home. Now, in my parents bedroom is another story. Because, like I said. I was aware of everything going on. I recall breaking into my parents bedroom just to be noisy, see what I can find. And, just so happen their TV was the only cable network. I was excited about watching the Playboy channel. Like most things I had to learn on my own. I guess I'll never know why this part of education wasn't important. And I can say the same about a lot of things I should've been taught at home. So ignoring it. Open the doors to explore, so the silent treatment never worked for me. I had to know. Watching all that sexual content taught me every thing and more. Maybe, it was a little to much for a kid my age. My very first sexual experience was with a girl. But I also tried it with a boy he was my next door neighbor. I guess feeling the need to keep it a secret was natural. How would I face my family, friends, and school mates about having sex with a boy? And being young at the time didn't have anything to do with having common sense. I knew I was living in a world that accepted the role of a woman and man in bed. Everywhere, I looked it was common. That's just how it was between a man and woman.

The same gender roles didn't feel acceptable growing up at the time. Being attracted to another man was considered wrong. I wasn't ready to share that secret part of my life. So things remained behind closed doors. Much to my surprise thing's changed, so I began to live, and I began to care less. It was here that I learned most gays feel more freely because the sex trade is a common practice in prison. Coming out wasn't difficult as I thought it would be at first. Hey it is. What it is. It's my life, so let me decide for myself. Who I am? And, so I began to live my lifestyle openly. There were some set backs at first, with rejection. It was like any other learning experience.

But I began to careless about the views of other's and embrace this new experience for myself. I had to accept myself first. Love myself first. And respect myself first before anyone else could.

The Marquette was a gay club located on the Westside. More like a hang out for the LGBT-Q community. That acronym wasn't establish before I came to prison. But it does educate people on the difference between such members from that community. This club was about five blocks from my neighbor hood, I'd walk some nights. A well know joint I frequented on the weekends. No matter what the vibe was I never left with anyone, I made sure the fun stayed inside the club. Maybe once or twice I mingled in the parking lot. I went there to enjoy the intimacy and social conversation. And the idea that the guy in the tight fitting skirt dancing. With the guy in the pin stripe suite was normal. And the couples over by the jukebox was just as happy together. I'm thinking nothing but men. Not weirdos, freaks, just men enjoying themselves. So there I was setting in a booth alone. While nursing a bottle of Corona watching this sissy blow me a kiss. That was just as normal also. But I would leave the club on such nights the same way I came feeling incomplete. Then upon entering my girlfriends apartment pleasing her sexually. Without fulfilling my own pleasure. I told myself something is definitely wrong with that picture. There I was in bed feeling both ruined and ashamed. I didn't want to face the facts. I thought right then and there that everyone would hate me. As much as I had despise myself. The lies continued to cloud my judgement. Small lies like the one I told my girlfriend when the phone rings. That was my partner from the job. But he sounds like a woman and is always calling my house. You need to stop playing she would demand. I'm not trying to start fighting Derrick but you seem to have an excuse for everything. If you're serious about us living together then you have to be more responsible. I would just listen to Frances feeling guilty. I'm a grown ass woman with a child. Living in my own apartment. And yes she had a point. To avoid being homeless. I stopped staying out all night cheating on Frances. But, the following week we fought again about the same thing. So that was it. I packed my things and left her. If that sounds familiar then I strongly suggest the same. Make a clean exit. Trust me. A man will get tired of hiding the truth. Soon or later things will come out. No matter how much you try to cover it up. That's if you tired of beating yourself up. You don't want to make the same mistakes I made. No way!

This is what opened my eyes. So much later. I would learn that all those chosen decisions were nothing but an illusion. Blinded by a reality and a condemned world. I grew up believing that there wasn't a difference between the two genders. They both shared an attraction for the same or opposite sex. As a man I was expected to be satisfied by both genders. No matter how much the world despise me.

CHAPTER 7

I see you still reading. That's wonderful because I'm not even half way into the story. The point is simply knowing Who you are? Will get you far in life. Along with other things, like knowing your purpose in life. So, I felt like a huge burden has been lifted. As I look around me each day. I notice the same vibe with brothers here in prison. Where most don't reach their fullest potential. Do you know me? Where did we meet? No and no. So, it's not our place to make past judgement because we're complete strangers. Yes, I'm talking to you. We're quick to find fault in others before looking in the mirror at our own flosses.

Getting to know each other shouldn't be so hard. But we choose a life that sets us apart. Instead, of allowing our differences to be nonjudgmental. Only for what cause we see today. It's no wonder why our social system here in America remains to be the worst ever. This is what made me do some long introspection of self. I realized I had to self love. Before, learning how to love others, regardless what bad decisions they made. I've made so many mistakes along the way. I can never look down on the next person, especially here in prison. Anyone can make an irrational decision, every once and awhile. We all are not perfect. No matter who you are. As men of habits, it is only natural. But, also possible to change as well. Sometimes I wonder why it took all those years to change and view the world differently. It's taken forever it seems from a prison cell. I guess because I've wasted so much time. When all I had to do, is do the right thing.

A dis-functional family gave way towards criminal activity and a lengthy criminal record. Not the least, having a life sentence. I'm currently fighting for a change. Time will do it. How we see ourselves should be determined by us, although that true self is hidden from us. As much as it is hidden from others. So who said, it's right for others to make such choices for us. Every day I awake with a constant reminder that this nation affirmed my ancestors three fifth of a person. That was a big issue then. But let's not get stuck there. We got miles to go before we can say, Peace brother! No matter what race, sex, or nationality we belong to. To many of us. See each other. As they see themselves. How can you judge me? Time for that shit to stop. Why I can't decide for myself, What I am, and What I'm not? I viewed it as the beginning of a new awareness of my own individual self and the world around me. Step after step, I tried to find out why my best efforts had been tested by problems.

I thought they could be fix. But my shallow understanding knew nothing. I spent so much time looking in the wrong places, and digging a whole deeper. For example, every day was a hustle, leading towards a jail cell later. I kept saying things aren't going to get any better. Or there wasn't a real reason to finish school. Please. An education wasn't going to put food on the table or clothes on my back.

So what else that world view included? Having to grow up in a repetitive society that I mistakenly believed held all the answers. If, I could just figure it out. Then things would be less of a problem. My determination to find the answers pulled me in so many dimensions.

I thought I'd been hoax. Into believing that being a black man was a curse. What struck me was the paste towards progress took longer than necessary. Plus the fact change wasn't happening fast enough. And although that side of me wanted to come out. I denied him that chance to control me. Because I knew the outcome. However, that didn't resolve the issue, every step forward was a dead end. I concluded that there wasn't an alternative that will make things better. So I took the plunge, again and again. This was a bleak moment.

Where I had to ask, Where am I going? How do I get there?

CHAPTER 8

In my life. I've discovered that survivors are not born in the moment of prestige and fame. They're born like dad and I. In the mist of toil and struggle. When there is nothing but dying hope. When they must stand up against the gigantic horizon of fear. In that moment there is surely doubts but they fight on anyway. Because some in born drive lives deep inside them. They trust in a belief they can not see, touch, or feel.

It seems like yesterday, when I was living a normal life. Having a youth full of energy, and was taught learning was important. At least it was a constant reminder having a basic education was needed for a promise future. And how far it could take me.

But, instead such lessons I rejected. Whoever said we are a product of our environment, lied. How can that be true? Just think. I wouldn't be here telling my story today. When I reflect back. I honestly believe we are fashioned by life experiences, even if you fall way side. But that's not an excuse, just get up and try it again. I been there done that a thousand times. And each time there was something to learn from it. Still to this day. I value knowledge and time over anything else because it's better knowing what to expect. Instead not knowing at all. And if I'm wrong. I have only myself to blame. Despite the misguided path I've chosen. I couldn't trick my mind to think there wasn't a different course I could take. Although, I put up a damn good front.

But, who was I fooling. I was raised in a privileged culture in which I'd become a disappointment. My father had wanted me to be nothing more than a normal son. Men had there place in this world. And it didn't involve picking up a gun, stealing, and breaking girls heart. He wanted to marry off his handsome son at the age eighteen. Evette was a single mother of one child. Living with her mother on the South side. She was supposed to be a recovering drug addict like my dad and his new wife. I learned later that she had way to many secrets and lies she tried to hide. However, her and I became close friends.

Have you ever heard birds of a feather flop together? I recall when Evette use to offer me sex for money, prostituting herself just to get high. Her own mother kicked her out the house at eighteen, because she got pregnant. She was an unfit mother neglecting the responsibility of raising her little girl. No way I was about to settle down with her. But fortunately, her mother took custody of the child. I eventually lost contact with Evette. I was to busy working and dodging trouble. By the time I realized it. It was to late, because I had got pulled over during a traffic stop. It was always something stupid like driving without license. So I let my father down after letting me drive his car. He took me inn to live with him because I had no place to stay. He helped me get a job working for the same company he was employed to. My dad couldn't bond me out because I had a warrant for my arrest in another county. I served three months in Fulton county, after leaving Clayton county for the traffic stop. Instead, my dad was cleaning his life up. He was married again, had a nice paying job, and living in a suitable home. Before I showed up on his door step. I was really impressed by him being drug free. I wanted to model my life just like him. James had done what I couldn't do. Change. I been treading the same road every since I was thirteen. Now at nineteen. I've yet changed my old ways.

It's not always easy having control. Something I wasn't good at, never being in control of my thoughts. And thinking negative will not get you far in life. I eventually got my mind back on track in jail, I hoped. Although the test was still out there waiting on me. No home. No money. No job. No nothing. I tried to make the best out of my situation. So I called my uncle Jimmy and told him I needed a place to stay.

CHAPTER 9

Jimmy and his wife Helen became my new family. They were happy about letting me move in with them. I figured since it was difficult looking for a job. May as well join my uncles landscaping business. It was doing pretty good, especially during the warmer season. As the months grew. I almost forgot about my real family. It felt strange, as if they no longer existed at all. In her own way. I guess Helen notice the distance between us to. She ask me one day. Why haven't you called your mother? It was obvious to me that my mama missed me and wanted to talk. And this was her way of helping her sister rekindle the ties between us. Did aunt Helen feel guilty about taking me inn? That thought was going through my mind. Because, I knew the two talked on the phone almost every day. Mama had to be concern about my current status living at her sister's house. Or maybe it was the fact,

Helen was tired of informing my mother about me. Well, I did call Mama and we caught up on some current events. She seemed very excited hearing my voice again.

I learned that Shan gave birth to my first nephew Jerrell. I was proud of my little sister being a mother. She was still living with our Mama. And I had already heard about Michelle's move to an apartment on the east side, living with her husband. And, she also would be giving birth soon. I felt selfish, being so distant from my flesh and blood. But I didn't want to entertain such thoughts at the moment. I was suppressing so many mix feelings, holding back guilt about my current situation. And although, I was running away it seems, from the past. For the first time I did consider my mama feelings. But no longer felt connected to my family. Where was my family when I really needed them? Somethings never change and that's how I viewed my life at the time. I actually felt better living with my aunt Helen. I was doing fine working, saving money, and feeling more free than I ever felt in awhile. During the winter season. Jimmy help me see that I had built up some unhealthy coping routines. The most obvious was falling behind my rent, due every month. So, along with my cousin we sold drugs to earn some extra money. I hated the winter because Jimmy's landscaping business wasn't doing to good. And I didn't know anything about saving money for a rainy day. So, sometimes I would search for jobs hiring in the Atlanta Journal Constitution news paper. The strangest thing happened one day. The work was still slow. But after a job we had pulled into a gas station before getting off Holcomb Bridge Rd., and onto Ga. 400. I happen to notice a huge sign Now Hiring plastered above the Regal Nissan car lot across the street. Before I could blink twice. I quickly apply for the job and got hired on the spot as a detail personal. Can you start tomorrow the manager asked me. Shit I can start right now, I thought.

For the next ten months or so. I held down that job traveling by bus.

It took me almost two hours to get there and back. Other than that I enjoyed the work. Plus, it paid pretty good

$11 an hour. I had the weekend off. I even had an option to make affordable payments on a new car. Which I didn't take advantage of the opportunity, because my engine blew up on the Toyota. Jimmy told me and my cousin. We just have to work hard doing honest work, if we plan on having a nice home. He was a clan of the Riley's. He was originally from Alabama, second to the eldest of ten children. My uncle and mentor. I looked up to Jimmy especially when he purchased a Nissan 300 ZX. That spots car was beautiful and very fast. I'd look at all the things he'd achieve. And say, I'll never live up to his expectations.

That's the part I don't like. It's the element we all don't like when we know the truth deep inside us. Some how with time. We grow older and more wiser. Our minds see things differently. Coming up in the world on both sides of the fence is a lesson it self. However, that doesn't mean we going to choose the good side. It's not time to act on it yet. All those delusional thoughts I would keep bottled up inside. And the reality always seem to turn out the same. I wasn't conscious of the fact that my life. Is a series of levels and each step involves it's own conflicts. My life had it's own value and limitations also. Why wasn't I aware of these things back then? I'll soon discover it later, but at that moment. I was unable to find my own way. Another thing puzzled me. Why all the blame ? What made me point the finger at others? Just, consider it. It's very obvious. I was hidden from my own self. I paid less attention in the mirror. I thought it was better putting the blame on them, actually an excuse to hide such guilt, pain, and shame.

CHAPTER 10

I was driving past South Fulton hospital. Heading to my aunt's house off Cleveland Ave. When suddenly, I notice a road block on Harris St. The same street I had to turn left on before pulling up to the house. I couldn't make a U-turn because the traffic was bumper to bumper, so I was stuck. Damn. I couldn't believe it. There I was behind the wheel of a stolen car, driving with no license, again. I just knew I was going to jail. And there was no other options but to accept. What was about to go down. I was arrested and bond over to the Fulton county jail. Because I knew that arrest would be the end of my car theft career. My court appointed attorney explains to me that they're going to revoke three years. I was shocked. I could hear my heart rate, especially when she said I might spend some time in prison. What do you mean prison? I'm just seventeen. I can't go to prison. I was flipping hard on this P.D for making a deal with the D.A. She could've talked them into giving me a lesser punishment. After regaining my senses. I looked at the bigger picture. If you can't do the time. Don't do the crime. I had no other choice. And for the next twenty four months. I was caged up like a damn monkey. Time seemed drawn out. Like it took forever for the months to end. And there were times I'd just shut down. Trying to avoid any kind of trouble, but if necessary fighting wasn't a problem for me. I was going to survive this journey.

In those youthful years. I tried to understand myself from a jail that I've temporarily made home. The process was a tremendous lesson in which I found several solutions in dealing with such repetitive problems. Coping with prison. I'm someone I don't want to be. So instead I wore a mask. That was easy. Whenever you are confine being placed among a group. You start to become just like them, rather being your individual self. This becomes difficult for anyone choosing to be their normal self. So who wants to stand out? It was easier for me to blind in with the crowd. In a way that no one would know my secrets, my personal issues, my fear of being in prison period. They call it being cool, but it wasn't.

Just imagine being buddy's with the enemy sitting down playing cards together. People you don't trust or know nothing about, so everything is supposed to be cool. Such behavior describes a person not really sure of themselves. Hanging on for the ride, not sure where the road ends. I'm talking about me. This was nothing but a act for me until I maxed out my time. I don't care how intelligent someone sounds. I pay close attention to the body language of the individual now. Your character is important. I never met so many fake guys, until I started coming to prison. Real recognize real regardless who you are. A person ask me, If you lost everything in this world. What asset will you have left? And sure enough, if we reflect on it. We will realize that our character is the only thing we have left. And I'm not saying it applies to everyone, you just have to feel people out before you can trust them. And keep in mind. Having a bad character is usually a learnt behavior that is taught by others.

••• ••• •••

On June 25, 1992. I was transferred to a diagnostic maximum security Jackson S.P. Where I was tested for several months. I heard all types of jail house rumors. That the prison confined some of the worse inmates convicted throughout 138 counties. One story I recall is the mysterious serial killer Wayne Williams. He allegedly was responsible for 60 missing and murdered children in Atlanta. From that alone I was nervous living among such inmates. Although the staff segregated high profile inmates from the general population. It was still unsettling for me. Their living unit was called Death Row. I even kept a distance from their hall way entrance. After, leaving Jackson I was calmer. I was then transferred to Muscogee County. With about eighteen months before my sentence expired. I was expecting a parole soon. This was a minimum-security county camp. No more than about 300 inmates at the most. Can you imagine being forced into labor. Instructed to work in a swamp full of dangerous reptiles. A known fact that everyone knew. Especially on Cobs detail. Well I wasn't a fool either. So to avoid it all together. I simply refused to work.

Well everything seemed fine. Until I received a letter from the parole board. They denied me because of my institutional conduct, disciplinary reports. This was also during the time Georgia took a bad snow storm, about 8 inches. The camp was closed for about a week. Which meant no free labor.

But, suddenly there was an emergency call. My detail was chosen for this important work assignment. I was both shocked and upset especially it being on a Friday. I couldn't refuse work anymore more either, because I didn't want my security to be raised up to close. We arrived at the location only 10 minutes from the prison.

I recognize the neighborhood as soon as we got off the bus. A middle class community where the street lead to a cul-de-sac. We had worked here before but not doing this. We were all instructed to remove debris, tree limbs blocking a very large sewer drain. In order to do that the cover had to be removed. By the time we all decided how to solve it. All seven men took a position reaching down, then on the count of three. We lifted it up, but something happened. The only possible thing was that someone lost their grip. And causing the heavy slab to fall hard. If you ever been in shock after a painful experience. Then you know the feeling. Not even a second later after regaining conscious. I just stood there staring at my right hand. It was deformed looking. The longest finger barely hanging on, and the finger next to it two inches gone. Everybody seemed as shocked as I was ,asking me. Man you okay?

CHAPTER 11

At the health clinic. I entered through the ICU receiving medical attention A-sap. As I laid there shackled to the bed. While the staff performed their duty. It occurred to me that this was the first time ever being admitted in a medical facility for a serious condition. Why did it have to happen in prison? Here I was just waiting surgery wearing tubes. Having a mental breakdown. I was having thoughts about my hand not being normal again. If, I wasn't in prison this incident would've never happened, period.

The feeling of being incompetent wasn't my style. I remember, refusing to take medication mama use to force me to take. Cold med's for a cold. I'd rather do away with all the medications for a recovery. No matter how much pain I was in. The doctor told me I'd be fine. After a few stitches my finger, will be normal again. Not a 100% but in stable. So for two days. I was on bed rest, stuck inside a room bored to death. A good thing about being in a hospital is watching TV. I also enjoyed being catered by all the fine nurses. It wasn't long after I was transferred back to the camp.

Then not even a week later. I was transferred to another facility due to my medical conditions. I'd expected it because the work camp only kept inmates that had no medical issues. I was still naïve about the penal system. How rules and policies govern inmates. I was told by other inmates that the state prison is more strict when it comes to authority. Even the inmates do their time differently. I learned very quickly that such rumors were true. When I arrived at Lee State Prison. Which was designed to house 800 inmates. The living units held 60 men and 5 men to a room. Unlike a county camp inmates here have restricted movement, on the general compound. If you was classified close security. Your chance of getting a work assignment outside the compound was impossible. Such was my case. I was still considered chronic care although my security remained medium.

The medication was some antibiotics for my right hand, and going to medical for therapy every week. I wasn't use to being stuck in the dorm all day. Here a typical day was waking up at 5:30 am. for breakfast. Staff inspection was between 9:30am-4:00pm. Including lunch and dinner. And if you're lucky you might get out side yard each day for 1 hour. Which I definitely took advantage of throughout the week days. No yard on the weekends. One of my favorite past time was playing pool inside the unit. This game was taught at an early age I believe when I was ten. My dad would take me to his friend's lounge in the city. His friend Thomas owned the place occupying six pool tables, two juke boxes, and a huge bar. The man had some serious money back in the days. On December 1, 1994 I maxed out my sentence from Valdosta State Prison. I walked down the steps of the CNN center downtown. My mama's car was parked on the curb.

Just like we planned, she was there on time, after I left the bus station. It felt strange being drove home by my mother. I walked out of her home, just to return again 3 years later. But with open arm's. Nothing mattered no more as long as I was now a free man again.

No. I couldn't do the things I use to do anymore. Especially, not in the presence of mama. Yeah. I thanked her for trusting and believing in me. Along with giving me another chance. She is a wonderful mother. And deep down inside. I thanked her for not running me down just to get me out of jail.

When I was the cause of disappointment and shame. And you know the funny thing is. I wasted all those youthful years being a bad ass. Throwing my life away to the system. I looked at her wondering. What kind of thoughts could be turning around in her head. Just hang in there son and pray.

But honestly I tried so hard hiding my inner thoughts. The same old song. Thought's about coming up with a hustle because I needed the money. Mama had moved on Pennington Place west Atlanta, the hood. I figured at the time. There wasn't nothing else to do. But what I been doing. Since I had no other support or connection in the streets. Don't get me wrong. There isn't a son. Who wasn't better off with a mother like mines. And don't know where I'd be without her. It's God plan. However, it took a lot for me to move back in with my mama. But some how we seem to get along just fine for now.

CHAPTER 12

Capitalism was a dangerous era for most blacks living in the metro Atlanta. Our farmer president Bill Clinton had just won the election. He found ways to put an end to the increasing crime rate. He focused on one of a few social, and economical disparities among the city. By employing more law enforcement policies, prosecutor's, and sheriff's. To make Atlanta more safer. This also, gave our politicians and law makers a permit to stricken laws and lengthen sentences. Therefore, placing a huge tax on the black communities at a cost of $80 billion a year. Also, during this time of inflation the city of Atlanta would be welcoming it's homage for the Olympics. Such sport event's would attract a tremendous population of wealthy consumers from all parts of the world. But in spite of this achievement. No wealthy person is blind to the needs of the poor living in the city.

In 1996 governor Wayne Gardner. Did away with institutions for higher learning in prison. No more opportunities offering a college degree for state inmates. He also removed the athletic programs using the weights to exercise. Our criminal justice system continues to be a growing epidemic against the idea of rehabilitation. It's no wonder why so many brothers reenter the criminal system. And, as law abiding citizens, along with victims of crime especially in our inner city. We should be protected by law. But how does our system reduce incarceration and over crowding? To ensure true change. We need to reform the penal system that, over criminalize, over punish, and over tax payers.

... ...

Making it on my own without the support of my family was a new experience for me. France and I had start dating. This young lady was a dark skin beauty in every way. Her nice looks and amazing character won me over. We connected on every level it seems from the beginning. We first met at a laundromat I frequently went to in the hood. I was still living with mama. And, although mama liked her, she didn't approve of our intimacy so soon. Boy you just met her. Little did mama know that my biological clock had been put on hold from those years I spent in prison. I guess the feeling was mutual. Because I didn't get no disapproval from France about my advances. She seemed to enjoy it more than me. And it wasn't long before we decided to live together, so I packed up and moved in with her. We had become inseparable, not sure if it was a weakness but I gave in quick. She had a seven year old son. We all lived in Olive Garden apartments on Fairburn Rd. together. Nothing fancy section -A housing. I felt like a burden since, I was still unemployed and the fact Frances was a single mother. Plus she wasn't making enough income working at Burger King. The unemployment check I received each month wasn't enough to help out. It only created more tension between us. So the little arguments we started to have was no surprise. If it wasn't about the dirty dishes in the sink, then it would be. Me yelling at her brat son all the time. And she was quick to let me know who apartment it was. We would make up just to get into a argument again. Eventually, things did change ounce I found a job at a temp service, she also got a better paying job. The temp service wasn't my style but I definitely needed the money. So I stuck with it. Frances was a full time secretary for a realtor company making a nice salary. But that didn't settle our on/off relationship.

At every turn. Steven pulled all the tricks, making it obvious he didn't like me living with them. Which his excuse was I'm not his real father. Sure enough our strange relationship grew more apart than anything. We couldn't seem to fix, what had been broken. And when a sister chose to use sex as an excuse. She has open up a door that will ruin any hope of keeping her man. I began to drift further away. Not caring about the way she was feeling towards me. So I did what came natural by finding pleasure and fun out side my home. Here I was again, looking at my reflection asking myself, Why such problems that challenge one's effort to make things better., only makes it much worse. But yet I saw no wrong, only a lesson for example. Some people just refuse to be accountable for making bad decisions. As if owning up to it isn't good for them, or doesn't benefit them then their not interested. We all heard it before. Frances was both hurt and confused I'd took the easy way out by failing her and Steven. Like a pre- nuptial we agreed that I take only what is mine. Not the things I gave her. Since she couldn't keep up the car payments for the Ford wagon we bought together, it belonged to me. Even though she put up a fuss. For what seemed like hours after I placed the last box in the trunk. You no good mother- fucker, she said as I quickly made my exit.

The first conclusion that struck me was that. The pace towards change was slower than it should be. We can neither turn forward nor back the hands of time. Which is impossible no matter the pace. Growing impatient with that pace. I began to look closer and discovered that the problem wasn't pace. But our human abilities to control self. I concluded that this self destruction raging against time wasn't nothing but an illusion. Therefore, we are struggling against something we can't control.

PART II

CHAPTER 13

Several years ago. When I was living a religious lifestyle. There were maybe twenty- two text books, on religion I owned. But only two were a constant read every day. The Quran and the life of the Prophet. Those two texts were essential towards understanding my life. Back in the days if the question was asked Why I was created? I probably would have answered a lot of wrong things. But I bet you. If the question was asked to any devotional brother from such religious group. The response would simply be to worship God. From a spiritual and social view such devotional brother beliefs are associated with his creator as well. There are many instructions on how a person should act and behave, towards treating others. Like the marriage between two people for example in Islam. Marriage is obligatory upon those who affirm their belief in God. Having sex out of wedlock is a major crime also. And the punishment could lead to death but only in countries ruled under the jurisprudence of Islam. It was concepts such as marriage I couldn't obey, especially after living a cultural here in America. I'm not the one to judge but let's keep it real. We got more night clubs, escort services, pornographic materials than any country on the planet. I can't speak for everyone just my own experience. The fear of God isn't going to stop me from telling the truth.

Yet, still the thought of having four wife's. Did raise some thoughts. And that's how I see it. Not black and white but what came natural. The human genetic make up of who we are. And what we determine. The way we should see the world. We all humans have a hidden desire of rage, joy, pleasure or happiness. But we don't necessarily act on them at times. These feelings are suppressed from our self as much as others.

Whether hidden or open their capable of failing us. Depending on the circumstances. We may entertain such thoughts without acting on them. Becoming our natural given ability that allows us to be conscious of those limitations through divine intervention. I call it spiritual inclination. The fact that a religious person relies on a faith, gives them limits to worldly thoughts when divine has already been decided in the matter. They call it the straight path. By repetitiously following different acts of worship God removes the evil (thoughts) that in it self enables the person a consciousness to do right. Now, I know you saying, What happened! Ok, I'll get to the point. As I quoted at the beginning. Being that I came from a religious back ground. Islam was already introduced at a early age but with a twisted belief. The truth came much later on here in prison. I guess you can say just like Malcolm X, similar experience upon knowing the truth about Islam. Al-Islam is the authentic religion. Apart from the dogmatic N.O.I established by Elijah Muhammad here in America

1930. From that point on knowing the truth. I got serious over a twelve year period living as a Muslim.

Although, I don't live that lifestyle anymore. I never read a text (Quran) that connected me to the essential nature in which the whole of humanity is deprived from a higher power. However, I'll always believe in my spiritual self. The biggest challenge is yourself. If God looks at the opposing self as the greatest hurdle towards having the proper belief to be successful. True. I'm going to share more on this subject in the following chapters, it's a process like anything we learn in life.

CHAPTER 14

I remember meeting back up with Frances. I was working as a stock clerk at Kroger's. She looked the same. It was obvious the new hairstyle had set her back some. But even the slight notice didn't hide her greatest assets. It's no wonder why I couldn't resist her beauty. And at every opportunity she flaunted her large breasts with pride. Nor did I hide my approval either. What's up? I asked, Frances with a smile. She returned the same before any words. Her face said it all. Ed working in a grocery store. How long have you been working here she asked, taking a closer step towards me. We talked about our past involvement. We both apologize for the way things happened, leaving off any personal feelings. That lead to a very disappointing separation between us. She was still with the realtor company. Steven was doing okay. But I thought maybe she had traded that gas gutter for a better car. I don't know if that was her way of inquiring about my Ford wagon, but I kept silent. It had gotten repossess anyway when I went to jail a year ago. At the least, we promise to keep in touch. I definitely wasn't interested in rekindling our relationship so I remained her friend. She did inquire about this new girl I was dating on the job. Oh, yeah you talking about Melody. Yeah we are together. I didn't have to ask who gave her that information, no doubt it was Sheila. Frances and Sheila had been friends for awhile even before we started dating and living together. Now everything made perfect sense.

I'd sometimes catch Sheila watching my every movie especially during lunch break. Normally couples would meet up in the break room at work. I recall flirting with her a few times but never took it seriously. Although the sister was fine. And besides Sheila was dating this guy at work. I definitely don't get down like that. How is your son? Damn, this girl knew all my personal business I thought. I mean this girl had me all figured out, it's no wonder why she decided to pop up at my job. She needed confirmation from what Sheila had been telling her. I didn't loose my cool. We just stared at each other, then started laughing. That's how we reunited and became friends again. I've had my share of women. What attract me the most was their honesty and loyalty. But you want find to many sisters who will keep it all the way real with you. And I'm not going to say it only applies to the women. This goes for both gender roles. For the most part, there are a lot of brothers here in prison who didn't keep it real. So to defuse things we have a draw.

··· ··· ···

During the mid 90's. I notice a progressive change taking place in the way women sought their men. The roles had switched almost completely. Now there were 10 women to every man. Women were getting their act together looking for Mr. Right to lead the house hold. I would go out to night clubs only to leave with more phone numbers

I could count. Or a sister to leave with me. I remember, hanging out at the Peacock along with some friends one night. We were sitting on the hood of my tricked out 79 Chevy watching a impromptu car show. In those days it was more action outside the club in the parking lot. When suddenly we all heard gun shots going off. Everybody scattered like ants ducking hoping not to get hit by a stray bullet. We listen to some girl who seen it, saying that four masked women. In a black van drove up to the entrance of the club shooting into the crowd. Leaving four people wounded and two dead. Now that was crazy. Like that movie Set it off.

It took me awhile to shack up with a sister again. I mean there is nothing wrong with moving in with a woman if that's the choice you take. Most men prefer the idea of a female being the bread winner, especially if she's receiving government assistance. Have you ever heard, It's cheaper to keep her? But in the long run. I bet you that sister is going to get tired of pampering your ass. For example, my aunt Joyce and her husband. They gave birth to two boys and sheltered their family for some very long years of marriage. She'd give her last dollar without asking twice. She had a big heart. And I felt sorry for her because my no good uncle took advantage of her. After Grady lost his job working for General Motors car plant. He later got hooked on crack spending his disability check every month on drugs. Leaving his wife to pay all the bills. But she was still determined to hold him down. Why? My aunt was a nice looking woman that could please any man. Instead, her love for her husband was deep. And what always bothered me was that. She would come home from work, cook, clean and tolerate the junkie's in her house. During this time. I'd just moved out of Frances apartment. I'd agreed to pay my aunt rent and help out around the house. Joyce place was on the East side. The cozy house had three bathrooms and two bathrooms on the top level. I was still working at Sai Motors as a forklift operator. My shift was from 3-11pm. But I was working through a temp service as a contract worker. So I was making only $8 an hour. The contract between the two companies were flexible which meant Sai Motors could end my sub contract. By simply hiring me on with them, which would increase my salary $12 an hour. I guess my life was making a change for the better part. On occasion there was a little tension because Joyce and I was the only two working. Being the oldest between me and my cousins. They didn't see me as often because I was either at work or hanging out with my friends. Sometimes Id give my aunt extra money. Oh Derrick you don't have to do that she'd say. Yes I do. You deserve it, ignoring her resentment and leaving it like that. On Sunday her cream fried corn was delicious. And why do women here in the South enjoy both cooking and listening to gospel Sunday morning? WAOK was the radio station. My mother played that same station like it was going out of style. They would say after each song. Thank you Jesus! As if the artists were being praised.

Grady did something that I thought was wrong. You know the

feeling. Thinking that everything is going well. That you are in control of the situation no matter what hurdles you have to get over. Then suddenly you get hit with a bomb. Well trust me I didn't see it coming. It never occurred to me that Grady was feeling a little insecure about me helping out. I over looked the things he wasn't doing for his family. I was simply helping. Although he claims the real issue with me wasn't that. But I broke his rules. Every since I was welcomed in their home they agreed I can have female guests. I'll admit sometimes they over stayed there welcome but it wasn't as bad as it looked. But I believe my cover was blown a few times to many. My room was directly across from my uncle bedroom. And I knew my cousins were snitching as well telling their parents that a girl had slept over from the previous day. They'd ask me, things like. What time she plan on leaving? How she getting home? Just maybe I was annoying the family peace so my uncle told me I got two weeks to move out. With no explanation needed. I just started looking for another place to stay. And luckily for me it came sooner than plan. What I didn't realize. How foolish I was to think that my promiscuous little mind could just have strange women over at odd hours. Without considering how it effected them. How self centered and selfish I was at the time.

CHAPTER 15

It was around this time. I conceived my first and only child. Derrick was born on May 5, 1997 at Piedmont hospital. Much to my surprise he took the likeness of his father more than anyone. I still recall the placid look from his mother laying there recovering from a difficult labor. Jacinta's grandmother also stood in the room gleaming with excitement. So, Ed you know what this means she said. Are you and Jay getting married? Jacinta and I had first met at her job Motel 6 a year ago. Like most young couples our age. The relationship always seem to evolve intimately before anything else. And the conclusion always be the unexpected mother pregnant with a child. No matter, how much she promised me she was on the pill it was my responsibility as a man to protect myself. Even against such risk like

STD, which is way more serious. But luckily that wasn't the case. But I remember the doubtful moments at Jackson where I was medical tested. Just imagine the thought of having unprotected sex with over fifty partners not knowing your health status. However, the case I didn't think it was a good time. To be raising a child, a huge mistake for me. I wasn't ready to be a father. And what made things even more complicated, I was alone in that opinion. Jay seemed to like the idea more and more. Everything had made sense the more I thought about it. Why I didn't see the signs sooner? The baby subjects would come up a few times, and often times she would demand my full attention in bed. Almost, begging me to make love to her. Before the big news came, I'm pregnant Ed.

Jacinta had expected a family. Something she didn't have as a child growing up. Her plan was to some day be the mother of a child, giving it an abundance of love. So this was one of our issues each time the subject was mentioned. I just listened, inwardly hiding my opinion. And not taking her seriously enough because I was cool with just the way things were. Having no attachments and doing what ever I wanted to do. Now, not protecting myself from such responsibility, did nothing but made my situation more complicated. It took me some time to accept this reality. How many young brothers you know openly and truly welcome fatherhood?

The impact of crime and abuse. Facing the full accountability of our actions is a necessary part of change. Unfortunately, as a victim of abuse. We're not always conscious of the unresolved anger. When you think of situations that get you upset in your present life, rather than looking for an alternative, perhaps all you see is failure. I'm taking about me. If you grow up with a very bad tantrum. You may think you are reasoning to the situations that is currently happening. I'm talking about me. But your more likely over burden with unresolved and covered up hate, pain, and anger of many years. Or a life time of resentment. And yes, I'm still talking about me. If we grew up in a family with drugs, neglect, or rejection our past is often repeated.

Playing itself out. Until the rage and pain from the past is resolved. And like my childhood experiences I mentioned earlier, for the later part of my life. I didn't have both parents while growing up as a child. Along with such signs of abuse occurring in the home. Many brothers like myself growing up without a father figure. While living in poverty poor conditions and being a delinquent repeat offender. Should know that this is a very common trait in today's world. And for those brothers growing up in the gang world. Where are the big homies now, since you joined. Even if you think such peers didn't have anything to do with you coming to prison. Think again. I advise you to look very close at my own personal experiences and tell me what you see. Look what happened to me. Now apply that to your own past and present situation. Prison is one of the most social places where men had been abuse as a child. I witness the signs every day. They had no idea how their former life had influenced their choice to head down the wrong path. Reflect back and you will discover that I was separated from a father leading to a dis functional family. This child neglect is real. A woman I believe can raise a son. But she can not teach him how to be a man.

Not only do the child lack a male role model. But also, the factors towards learning correct behavior from a positive perspective. Like iron sharpens iron. If negative behavior is all that the child knows from his peers. Then naturally they will believe it's cool to act that way. Childhood abuse was my case. Therefore it's not the child fault. So the fact remains childhood abuse and neglect is the major cause why our prison system is over rated today.

We are a long ways from the Cosby show era. That television sitcom, touched the soul of black culture. Weather you was raised in poverty or wealth. The same act JJ Evans brought to the screen in Good times. Those black comedy shows in the 80's-90's defined the very essence of how our life's depend on the stages of conflict. Our life's start as good. In touch with our inner free will. As a child our unconsciousness is very vulnerable in which the basic needs must be given through parenting. However, consciously growing as an adult. Our needs for safety, compassion, and love are met. In order to prevail any emotional life experiences. The child has to grow up and become an adult. Then that adult remains stable, lingering with a purpose to be successful and happy in life. So laughing is good and healthy. We can not be truly happy men's on a weak structure such as that vulnerable child who never got it's needs met.

When the man in our life's can't stand on its own. Lacking true love, courage, and affection. We continue to age but our personal growth and development is left behind. Our efforts to act naturally and behave normally is useless. Therefore, we build walls up, hold back, and make petty excuses for ourselves. Such walls of toughness, walls of hate all to protect that innocent child inside. Who's hiding and to afraid to face the real world. My understanding of who I've become feels great. I'm learning more and more. As a mature man in all aspects of life. Anyone can recover from ills of self. We continue to do things right at the start. Our willingness to be the best we can be, simply believing we can past the test. And to the hurting child within us. There is a unconscious pattern repeating itself. The same negative behavior that has made your life unsuccessful over the years. Groups are more immortal than individuals.

CHAPTER 16

In the previous chapters. I briefly talked about how spirituality can influence a person's life towards living righteous. Not only our spiritual but being genuine about increasing your understanding in life, which I will discuss in this chapter. Not after living in so much darkness and ugliness. At the age 28 serving 9 life's and 30 years. I was more than ready to change my game plan. I didn't see no other alternative in the way my life had turned out. It was going to be a long time before seeing the real world again. Both of my parents was more than willing to support my efforts. Although it took mama awhile, grieving her sons current situation, eventually things got better. She found another job. Her former job at Alonzo YDC seemed unmanageable, being around so many juvenile offender's. Even working as a dietary aid was a constant reminder of Derrick. Our communication by writing helped some prior to me being sent off to prison. Unfortunately, at Jackson inmates visits and phone calls aren't allowed. So I had to write a lot of letters to family and friends. I gradually learned how to spend my time doing things connected to my new life. It was almost like riding a bike all over again, never fretting the challenge. Much thanks to my familiar past living in a jail cell.

Learning from an experience can get you far in life. A perfect guide. My dad I suppose took the news pretty well. If there were any resentment the old man didn't show it. But, I sense the disappointment in his face. What father wouldn't be emotional let down after loosing their son to the system. Which gave me a more better understanding about my own coping issues. Because seeing my son in visitation took a lot out of me. There was no denying it. We all felt the pain of being genetically separated. Depending on the prison visitation privileges. I took advantage of family pictures taken as well during visiting hours.

Still to this day. I never understood the reason why Jacinta never brought our son to come see me. We were friends at the time, and kept in touch writing each other. A few times I did inquire about it. I even sent her the proper forms so she can be approved for visitation. But, her excuse was always she had to work and being a mother of three kids took up most of her personal time. She had two girls after our son. Kamara and Kashaya. I had no legal grounds so I left it alone.

But I do believe it was revenge from our past involvement.

••• ••• •••

On different levels. Learning is very fundamental. Understanding with reasoning how well a person act on learning. And this method may be difficult for a brother here in prison living under so much peer pressure, but it's possible. I have met some very intelligent brothers who lack in their belief system because they can not act on knowledge. Especially, when the rules are from a higher source. Or simply obeying those who are in authority over them. You would think they would be subordinate but they choose the very opposite. Either way if the knowledge is applied right, it can mold your character. So, yes it's a process. Let's be honest. A brother's failure to take personal responsibility for his wrong doing isn't going to work. He can forget about the prison warden putting in a recommendation on good behavior. Ask, yourself How can I help reduce the rate of masincarceration in my prison? What can I do to better improve my re-entry skills? I've learned a lot just watching these brothers in here. If we want to be physically free from our temporary jail cell. I suggest you to spend as much time needed doing some internal inventory on your current situation. We must pay real close attention to our own personal growth. Any structure without a firm foundation, can not with stand a storm. When I took on the responsibility of educating myself. I felt good about how it changed my perspective, providing the right understanding and helping me cope with prison life. One thing for sure this place will promote violence. It's full of destruction. However, the case it doesn't mean you allow it to distract you. No. It means you distance yourself from the foolishness. There are so many lessons to learn from your past and present. Like being someone I'm not opposed to the person I am now. Or feeling guilty for what you have done to someone else. It applies to us all.

Such guilt develops when everything thing you ever own. Has been taken away from you. When your values (clothes, cars, money) have been stripped away. You want back what is only natural, because it's all you got to survive. Places like prison is where we don't feel that natural freedom. Although, we are mentally free. We are physically locked up and limited to feel love, affection, or being our true self. With a limited reasoning we come to believe we're never going to attain a new trial or make parole. And, no matter how hard I try there seems not enough time to get things done. I was amazed to see some efforts being made but not much.

If we don't sincerely work on our wounds, pains, and sufferings. Our life becomes inevitable attach to inconsequential matters. And trivial circumstances each vying for our attention. We can become so involved with materialistic things. That we leave off our inner relationship (self), rejecting conflicts within us. A few years ago. I came across an article in a magazine reporting Oprah along her guest's. Tripper Gore and Ice T. Is Hip Hop MC's failing to serve as role models for young children? Who hear their music? Ice T's response was that. The job of the artist isn't to examine his work, but to report from the front lines of living. His world is a cruel one he accepts. An unwanted one he admits but he isn't in no position to examine his experience. When you take stock of yourself. You will begin to notice a connection between yourself and other's circumstance coping with prison life. But what sets us apart is that inner thought that enables us to become a better person. And no matter how much I loved rap music then. No one can convince me. That Ice T had promoted a positive message towards our young brothers in that era. Which still remains a trend among such artists today.

CHAPTER 17

The good news is that it is doable. If, we stay focused and sincere. Maintaining a balance schedule so that our basic needs are met each day. This course takes a lot of planning and hard work. Just imagine how corrupt life would be. If we don't set limitations upon the things we depend on. I recall being a very lost soul, prior to picking up the piece's and cleaning out such negativity that incite me to do wrong. We must create means that incline towards flushing out less important matters. And focus only on those immediate tasks that stunt progress. I discovered a passion for reading and writing. Poetry is one of many works I've done here in prison. I enjoy the feeling of thinking outside the box. This outlet has open some doors to opportunities like freelance literature through a non profit news paper I established. And writing skits for my family personal website, intended to keep us connected. Unfortunately, I lost over 100 pgs. of poetry I wrote. Which is to disappointing to share the story. I get upset just thinking about that lost. I simply, had let someone read it but they never returned my property. Yet I've managed to save some.

I was told fear is the beginning of knowledge. And I believe it too. It can change your views about life in general, from a social standpoint. Or perhaps finding out the truth about things we don't know. It allows us to see life for what it truly is and how natural we react and behave toward others. We should all know the difference because it makes us moody at times or just tired of the way things are. No matter how high or low our admiration may appear. We all have something in common we can not over look. We must cooperate to meet the challenge of understanding life. And living up to its values and principles. Even, if it means we have to make sacrifices for the better good. Such changes like transitioning our current location, request a transfer to another facility that offers vocational training. We have to give up our ego and arrogance. Concentrate only on our current situation while meeting the challenge of understanding life.

There are three types of men in the world. I would like to describe the first. A man who self indulge in everything he do. Without any remorse about the pain and affliction he has caused on others. Or himself. The second is a man that lives a double standard life. He isn't sincere about the life he has chosen through his actions. But yet still claims to be genuine. The last is a man that knows himself consciously seeking to improve his understanding. And sharing what he attains with others. The second type of man. Is where a majority of brothers are at, especially here in prison. They struggle with the increasing tasks of dealing with their own failure, knowingly. It is a unmanageable life. You find yourself in a situation. A situation, it seems almost impossible to improve. Or control the way your life is heading. Believe it or not. The same principals you fail short to get here in prison, is the same controlling world. Prison is just a smaller population of people.

The changing of man to choose that destiny depends on him. Cons like me. Who have been serving a long stretch. Can accept failure as a sign to change their game plan. But regardless what crime. Or how much time you got sent away. Your not a failure unless such down fall is the limit you set yourself. There are many ways to past time productively. By getting a G.E.D, vocational training in a skill, self help programs etc. I recall being at this private prison a few years ago. They offered a k-9 class, training real dogs. Plus the inmates were allowed to live, along with the dog they trained in the same dorm. Quite naturally, there were certain qualifications, for enrollment because it served as a means for good credit towards getting parole. But the opportunity was there matter fact, you became the dog owner for six months. I mean it's what you make it to be. Like the saying, It's not about the time. But what you do with the time. I never been extraverted. I always keep to myself. But in here I had to learn how to be sociable at times. How to connect with others. Being an over achiever since childhood played a huge factor. So I didn't have to fit inn, with them. Fortunately, for me it came natural, having something others lack. Being a mentor for brothers in here teaching them basic skills in boxing, arts, wood crafting and their spiritual journey. It's fun if your heart is in the right place. What black civil rights leader in our history didn't get a high school diploma? Malcolm X's failure to attain such honorary was the case. But, his self determination in prison didn't prevent him from seeking and acquiring a higher learning. Reading and writing itself can support your emotional and spiritual well being. Given a free pass. The prison library is a source of expanding your history and rational intellect. The benefits of doing time well. Provides an abundance of peace, humility, and self esteem. Or better yet, a decision making from those who are responsible for your release. Let's not walk out with the same repetitive mind that caused us to be here. Time is very valuable. By spending your time wisely. You break that cycle thus, freeing your mind. And in fact, our prisons today. Have become so violent that any efforts making a change seems impossible, but it's not. We just have to work harder at it. What I suggest is finding peace of mind in segregation SMU. So that you will be more in control. We suppose to be mentally free by learning how to do time. Don't let time do you!

CHAPTER 18

Now here is the down side. Knowledge is power true enough. But, it can also be useless, if not practice or used the wrong way. Have you ever heard. You can lead a mule to the well, but you can't make it drink. Every thing we consciously do. In order to benefit us, must first be done with pure intentions. When the mental is at work. We are focus and relax with very little distractions around us. Keeping in mind during such process, our visions become more alive and a perception which is our very own. This is important if we are serious about crossing the finish line. That's why the pupil Elisha. Became a great leader in his time, and heeding the instructions of his successor Elijah. As sure as the Lord lives and as you live. I will never leave you. Not, only did he attain a high position in what Elijah taught him. He was willing with determination to act upon knowledge. And understanding while remaining Elijah's student.

This is the balance we need. If we trick our mind to think it's possible living life rejecting instructions. Without failure or self destruction. Then we may as well choose prison as our permanent home. Look at it this way. They have a law that is punishable by repeating a felony over and over again. If the crime is a serious felony a brother will receive LWP upon his second serious felony. This recidivate law was intended to reduce the crime and incarceration rate. But, years later it has served as a mass incarceration tool. Along with the increasing unsafe and inhumane conditions of the prison system. Costing tax payers $80 billion per year, that's $53 per day to confine a person. So, now the politicians are saying. Oops, we made a mistake, let's design a new program that will correct that problem because the old one failed. Do our family and friends get a refund on their annual tax return? By having the proper understanding. We can simply, debilitate our situation and circumstances. Upon such injustice, rather impair our mental and spiritual potentials. Time can be used in a good or bad way. It's up to you. This same principal applies to parents also. Being ignorant to law is not an excuse. Although parents may have strict work schedules that demand most of their time away from home. Or after a long busy work week. Your family, comes first in any situation making time for them so that such basic necessities are met. Especially, those single mothers having more than one mouth to feed. If, you're so occupied with work, that neglect healthy relationships with family. Or enjoying your job so much it causes you to forget about such needs at home. Distractions pulling you this way and that way. Making it impossible to have a balance life. Then parents I strongly suggest you to take control of your life.

An unbalance life. Describes a life that is unjust, leading to a dead end. Also idling time, socializing and mixing with bad company. Is very unhealthy for you. It's a situation where you can't find a peace of mind. Although, having a strong balance is tough I'll admit. Looking back at my own experience here in prison took time and hard work as well. But some brothers are aware of this personal management problem but rather remain attach to gratification. If we look close at the mind. We can easily confirm. That our mind is capable of solving any problems we may encounter in life. No matter how difficult we may think it is to solve. Being ignorant isn't an option either. The truth is that the present condition of our lives will never change. Not, until we reform that, within us. And, again brothers the good news is right before us, if we're willing to follow the lessons. Create your planning. Define meaningful projects that will take it beyond these walls, leading towards a career on the other side.

All personal management begins with self. Make sure to include a range of spiritual, mental, and physical tasks each day. Exercise positivity by thinking before acting on it. Stay away from distractions, procrastinating, and idling time which results a lack of concentration. And, oh, yeah try not to over do to much. Balance.

CHAPTER 19

Naturally our basic needs. Such as living in a safe and secure environment in most cases is put at risk. It brings a type of fear that undermine any change. I've been there many times before. It was a very uncomfortable position to be in but fortunately, I remained humble. Not giving in to such repetitive issues. The same can be said about our desires. Always wanting things like drugs, alcohol, clothes etc. But, not being content with the things we already have. There are many reasons for this compulsive behavior. Some research say that there may be a genetic tendency toward alcoholism or drug user's but I don't agree. Any addiction I believe is a learned behavior, allowing our minds to be plaque with negativity. Take a look around you. We see nothing but a bunch of brothers in our living units divided among each other. Notice the group getting loud and debating about Who is going to win the Super bowl? Pay attention to the brothers acting obnoxious because the staff took their store this week. And, the two brothers in a stand off, ready to kill each other over a bet. Such behavior patterns are common here in prison. I've witness well over 60% of the general inmate population addicted to drugs alone. About 20% of them were user's prior coming to prison.

Until the inner self is restored with true values. Only then he/she can begin the process of healing. I know these things. I've watched brothers join gangs, giving them a false identity they so unconsciously choose for themselves. All because of blind following someone else. A known fact, with our young youth picking up bad behavior from their peers. I've seen other factors like fear being the reason brothers join gangs. Fear is also a behavior caused by the lack of being confined in a safe and secure environment. That feeling alone can entice a person to act out violent, because they fear for their life. Which isn't a bad idea protecting yourself. There has been times, when I had to own a shank. Along with that learned behavior, even when you have gotten rid of the old baggage. Such new codependence just get transferred from one thing to another for example. You give up gambling but set in front of a t.v watching ESPN 24-7. You give up using drugs but crave eating food all day. To remedy any addiction means leaving off and refrain. In order to rid the wrong. When we don't seek alternatives to make our situation better for ourselves so that we can live freely. We only hurt ourselves. Why do we prefer the former over the later parts of living? However, if you have made amends, for the better part of living right. Then congratulations on a fine job because we all deserve to feel free.

••• ••• •••

I believe it was the year 2011. I was laying on my bunk thinking about the first time I ever been assaulted here in prison. I was attacked by two brothers and left severely wounded beaten and temporarily unconscious. The only thing I remember after the attack was slowly raising myself off the floor. I felt a massive pain all over. Instantly the guards rushed me out the door. I was resisting while the red fluid tricked down my face, knowing I was hurt bad. Yep, it was ugly. And getting revenge was my only concern. But, fortunately I was quickly rushed to the hospital and treated for my injuries. The most damage was a concussion to the head along with an open scare requiring six stitches. Also a permanent closed nostril making it difficult to breathe.

This happened during a very difficult time. Where I had to ask myself. Who am I? I pegged myself to be ahead of most brothers. There I was searching for the answers I thought I'd already knew, but was wrong. A question most of us never considered asking, Who am I? Really. The first thought came to mind. Could this just be another sign showing me a continuation of my former life experiences defining who I am, based on my present situation. The second thought, was that how often do I doubt. Who I was before this incident occurred. When I came to realize is that. All I was doing is defining myself through a reflection of my former self in the mirror. As if searching for the right gear to wear for a special occasion, but still not satisfied. There is nothing I can do to satisfy the outer appearance. No where in prison is safe today. This can be a challenge using your time to get know who you really is, spending quality time getting a better understanding. But, isolated units do provide some means of safety. SMU is a single cell. Normally such housing is designed for people who need protective custody. The special men unit provides more advantage for inmates to feel in control and less controlled by others.

If you're a introvert like myself. Or even if you have a upcoming max out date or parole month. I strongly suggest you to request SMU housing. Prison is far from being humane in many ways. No society it seems for that matter. And the next step should be working on removing that fictitious identity before you get out of prison. However, living with limited beliefs about who you are for example, I am a gang banger. I am a rapper. I am a football player. Or just plain lazy. Such labels and roles describe trends that are associated with the world. But does that cover all aspects of a man? So why is the behavior carried out 24-7? Have you ever noticed a behavior within yourself, that is unlike your outer appearance? Just maybe it started at grade school. Or it could've developed on your fist bid. Let me talk about the later sub personality because I know most brothers can relate. It happens to the best of us. But rarely do we understand the meaning of a man.

So we struggle to act out this role we play. Instead from a natural standpoint pattern it is being responsible for ourselves, family, and child. Providing love, affection, and guidance that goes way beyond the mask, we often wear. Young black men grow up in our inner cities with the cruel realities of limited opportunities. Which may affect the house hold. Such opportunities in education, employment, housing etc. among minorities is often a huge disadvantage. This kind of environment all play a part in reducing our positive expectations for a promise future. As well as our feelings about being a good man.

Parenting is important. Any child can attain true values. If given the chance to be nourished from a loving, caring, and compassionate father. One who produce and take care his children. All this is manageable from a mature parent who knows their self worth. They're willing to meet the challenge. He/she seeks to counter act any negative social influences that may under mind a child's future. But, unfortunately very few of us was granted the privilege being raised that way. However, some of us did have loving parents. We were brought into the world with unique personality traits and a beautiful free will. And also, gifted with guardian's who taught us right from wrong as kid's. So, the government don't raise children. Parents do. They say we need better school systems and programs, maybe that's true but institutions don't raise children either. Parents do. As a Parent. Your duty is to govern your own home. As a parent your duty to educate your kid's in the way of spiritual interactions. You get the first act of rebellion. So have a 1on 1 with them. Kindly explain to them their issues, and a simple method to resolve it. It's a chance they may not take heed but it's important to always make them feel, verbal communication is important. Or perhaps it's possible they may accept your advice, and do the right thing.

We all face a dramatic moment at some point. That's only natural. And it's our living experience that makes us humans, so if we learn from them. We begin the process intended no matter the age, nationality, or sex. Whatever the case, the world as we know has changed but what about you?

CHAPTER 20

Now I want to extend the subject a little. Let's look at this discussion from another angle. Because we have so many opportunities to become better than before. This only applies to those who know themselves. Another thing I discovered about our individual power to change our conditions. Is thinking positive about spending whatever amount of time here in prison. Is viewing crisis in a good way. This word crisis means a basic change of status in a persons life. A time of crisis can apply to most everyone in prison. This suggest that certain conditions of confinement may affect a person's fear, insecurity, and low self esteem. And is often the case in severe situations and circumstances. Further, causing mental health issues. The later can result in a persons long prison sentence. By the time they reach twenty years, a bad crisis is all they know with limited opportunities to recover. Oppose to the persons self will and determination to do what's right. And trying to improve his conditions in prison. Most brothers is content with certain addiction's further clouding their judgement. I read some where that 75% of people entering prison are drug and alcohol addicts. That is beyond reality. All of addicts time is occupied getting high or drunk. I have lost some really cool brothers because they chose that path. There is no self awareness, self esteem, or self motivation. His whole view is aligned with welcoming a bad stage of crisis.

This, crisis can be a turning point. No matter what the situation. It can be a positive change throughout the course of spending time in prison. When time I believe is considered a means for fulfilling ones priority in life. Strange in itself and with a limited selection. The prison system offers an opportunity for learning skills, jobs, and building such re-entry education. Before returning back home. Depending on the crime judges can impose mandatory classes like AA (alcohol anonymous), Anger management, Family violence, etc. for such crime committed prior to release. It was interesting to learn that this place can have a tremendous impact on the mind, body, and soul from a positive stand point. But it's up to the individual to make amends. As I look around me. Here in my living unit for example. The scene is almost moving to write about. The more time past it seems these brothers are rushing to meet their maker for real. No one can make another person change. Have you ever invested time in someone positively, and they just wasn't ready? I've been in that situation to many times to count believe it or not, and it only made me more compassionate. Like many of our courageous leaders who dedicated their life's towards attaining knowledge and teaching it to others. Yeah, it's discouraging being in the mist of so many lost souls. But my efforts will never change making a difference.

When you use your time for an opportunity to grow healthy and spiritual. You are on the right path. You become less concerned about what's behind you, and more focused on what's in front of you. Living for the future. You can continue working on the task before you, feeling good about such achievements. People you have inspired along the way leading by example. If you want to understand yourself. I suggest you start reading spiritual literature. Such texts like the Bible, Quran etc. where all humanity first began. It's better if you have someone who can interpret these references in order to get a more clear understanding. What was the meaning of the message? Why it was revealed at the time inspired by God? All knowledge is deprived from divine inspiration. Sent down from heaven revealing to prophets instructions for mankind. I truly believe serving my God is associated with my purpose and identity. Instead, in today's world. We see a majority of people putting money, cars, and materials before their God. All people are born spiritual beings. With all or the similar personality traits that made us Mike, Jeff, Kathy and you too. We each have a free will that decide right from wrong, true from false, rather we act friendly, mad, or just stupid. The choice is up to you alone. If we don't stop. Turn the noise down and listen. We will unconsciously choose reliving a repeated cycle of our inner conflicts that debilitate national human progress. Mentally you can advance your reading skills. Put aside unspiritual courses of history according to man made ideas and theory's about life.

Back then they named such people rational thinkers. Who were very intellectual about life on all aspects. They were leaders helping industrialize towns, cities, throughout the world. I further extended my research here in prison. African American literature is one of my favorite subjects. I enjoy reading and studying about our black culture. In my opinion it's better for parents teaching their child at home, rather depending on public school text books.

Even in an advance high school I discovered my social study class lack such history records. Those text books that were used then in the 80s focused more on other races, culture's, and heritage's than black's. African American history is basically a record of conflict between integrationist and nationalist power in politics, economics, and culture.

Such leaders like W.E Dubois, Fredrick Douglas, Marcus Garvey, and James Baldwin. Between the 1900-1930's, Harlem New York became the most prominent black city in economics, and political development. Then there were black literary authors, biography books I've read along the way.

Mostly in the prison library. I recall a lot of hours spent there in the mist of so much information to choose from. Have you ever heard getting a disciplinary for being in the library? That is how much I valued my time, seeking knowledge and understanding. I know you remember the basketball center Kareem Abdullah Jabar. He wrote the book Black Profiles in Courage. Most content he used talks about ancient blacks on a international level such pioneers, settlers, and explores bold achievements. His thesis that ancient slavery was never about race, but in fact the African modern slave trade. Did not appear in America until Spain and Portugal discovered it. Every family and house hold should read these biography books: Make me want to Hola by. Nathan McCall, Revolution by the Book by. Jamil Alamin, Malcolm X by. Kofi Natambu, Mentality and Morality of American history by. Jamal R. Rashid, African man lost from his own reality by. Sharif H. Nadir, and Slave in the family by. Edward Ball.

CHAPTER 21

The impact of crime. Can effect not only the victim involved but also the family of the person that committed the crime. Most of us know deep inside that we have wronged someone else, especially those close to us. After being sent away to prison this time for a Armed Robbery. It was awhile before I faced guilt and self forgiveness. I don't remember exactly what the date was. But it was around the time I was living a religious lifestyle, learning more and more how to serve my creator. No part of a man's life is better than the next I believe. This is my second time in prison. And I'm not ashamed to admit. All the years in here hasn't been easy. But, now I realize how important it was for me to reveal the truth. Holding it all in wasn't going to work. Such pain, guilt, and shame will continue, no matter how much you hold back. At every given opportunity you'll be tested. But, knowing it and really living out the experience is two different feelings. I swear I'll never hide from myself again.

On October 1, 1999 the guilt and shame weighed on me so much, that remorse for the victims was far from my mind. I denied any involvement for robbing the subway restaurant. I guess, the reality of what was happening to my life. Didn't register until I receive the lengthy punishment in prison. I was still driven by pride, unforgiven, and anger I was in jail. I was even more upset with myself. When I discovered the investigators lead to my arrest. How stupid of me, that mistake caused me to loose everything. It's crazy how criminals don't think about those things before doing wrong. It's always after the fact. It don't hit home run until everything is gone. I was loosing a fight for my freedom. I remember, the D.A's offer 20 to 10 years. And my public defenders advice telling me to take the guilty plea. I told her she must be crazy. I just couldn't spend the minimum of ten years in prison. I was in denial hoping to get a different outcome by going to trial. I lost that decision in 2000. But was still not ready to forgive myself. So I lost again in 2001, through a direct appeal. Then after that huge disappointment I was denied several motions in the lower court, Motion for new trial, Motion to vacate sentence, Motion for sentence reduction etc. I also, petition to the courts on such grounds for miscarriage of justice, ineffective assistance by the appeal attorney and more harmless errors the trail court made. After so many efforts. I wasn't going to give in but my guilt was eating me up. And like my former experiences, I started sharing my feelings with those close to me. Something I just knew I had to do. Not until around 2009. I decided that living a spiritual life requires true forgiveness before prayers can be answered. My lessons was telling me that this applies to those you know like family, friends, neighbors etc. As well as those victims you have wronged. And although I wasn't face to face with those I wronged. I still knew it was the right thing to do. But, what felt strange was building up the courage, confronting these issues in order for the healing process to work. I was doubting myself. Thought's like is it or not the right thing to do. The determination took some time, yet I came up with an idea. It made perfect sense because taking responsibility is required towards healing. Fortunately, for me I wasn't no longer suffering from absent of guilt. This new feeling made me think about all those other moments. Not owning up to my mistakes. How can I have personal relationship with God, without being completely honest? This feeling was connected with my family and friends as well. So whenever I wrote a letter to my parents. I was sure to pure out my forgiveness and deepest apologies for letting them down. My sister's received the same. And at every opportunity I would write, call and request visits from them. Even if I didn't get a response from them, I didn't care. As long as my intentions were sincere, nothing else mattered at the time.

Being that it felt only natural. Especially, in my case considering the support from both parents. Where would I be if it wasn't for them? Some people I've met are totally disconnected from guilt. There are crimes where the victims entire family is brutally murdered, psycho paths. Such crimes are committed without conscience where the person has no feelings, guilt, or remorse for that matter. Things could've been a lot worse for me. I see these behaviors all the time in here. They seem isolated from anything natural. I knew everybody's experience in the real world shaped who he was in prison. I learned that there are layers to men. You expect the good. But later you find out he doesn't deserve your time. This is a common thing that I had to adapt to in order to survive. I begin to see my views differently because I was evolving every day. You can't hold on to those experiences or you become bitter. Every day is a beginning. You look for the good in people. Have you ever seen Silence of the lamb?

Hannibal Lector was the leading actor in that movie. A ruthless psychopathic killer. His behavior showed a lack of extreme conscience rooted from severe childhood neglect and abuse. I thought about the impact after the robbery. I spent days and nights in my cell looking back. I made that mistake more so because I needed the money. Nothing else. I remember, at trail the faces of emotional, pain, and disappointment. I never thought about victims impact up to that point. I regretted it all now. Why did I do this to them? It wasn't supposed to happen like that? Even during my sentence hearing I listen to the woman remark, I hope he dies in prison.

··· ··· ···

In September 2012, James Robinson died. My dad's diabetes had gotten worse leading to the last moment's of his life. At the time I was at Wilcox State Prison. A medium security prison. I was working in the kitchen when the news reached me. The guard instructed me to report to my counselors office. From that point on I knew something wasn't right. I quickly left almost in a sprint, getting close to the front a gut feeling that it wasn't good. On a Saturday! Upon seeing my counselor on the phone ushering me to have a seat. I then heard him say, Yeah, your son just walked in Ms. Robinson. I felt a relief wash over me. But immediately, after putting the phone to my ear. Something bad had happened to my father. Another terrible death happened later my aunt Gloria. She had a stroke. Then after that aunt Helen died. Her cause was an impairment to the central nervous system. I believe triggered by alcohol abuse. Despite other losses while in prison. It's a reality of victimization as well. In the following chapter. I will discuss how self forgiveness is important. In connection with one's guilt thus necessary in order to heal and live a healthy life.

CHAPTER 22

Self forgiveness is a individual process that I had to learn. It was achieved through several methods. I have chosen by sharing them with you. Like the previous chapter explaining how such experiences provided time and thoughts toward getting were I'm at now. For that reason alone, I'm thankful. I have to thank God for forgiveness. I truly believe self forgiveness isn't possible without first being forgiven by God. By openly admitting the truth. And the truth about your feelings towards those you have wronged. Yeah it takes courage to admit your short comings, trust me. We all make bad choices and decisions. Rather, than admitting the truth I chose the hardest way. By denying my past guilt. If I could do it over again. I would but I can't which was a lesson I had to learn. All I could think was the fear of going back to prison for 10 long years. If I knew what I know now. I wouldn't be here telling this story. My journey towards making amends and viewing my situation differently. Seems as if the change happened over night. I remember joining a community of brothers. Who were involved with helping others learn about God. I was probably the youngest member at the time. This was at Smith State Prison 2001-2023. Although, my spiritual maturity had given me a position in the group. I was lacking in behavior. And it really disappointed the elders seeing me get into trouble. My biggest issue was being told what to do. I never was good at that. Even from a spiritual standpoint I always chose to be extreme in my views. I remember being wrote up for not shaving my beard. It was against the rules if you didn't have a profile to wear a beard. And it had to be no longer than 8 of an inch. Depending on the staff or guard, they allowed my community to freely wear beards. But, there were 12s, a nick name we gave to staffs who were strictly by the books.

Although, developing such coping skills took some time. I was eager to change. I wanted to leave prison a different way than I came in here. I tried so hard. I perceived the world around me below the knowledge of my religious beliefs. And that made me a target. I remember the times when a 12 would free pick me out of a crowd. No matter how much I'd protest about them accusing me of doing something wrong. It was useless because I had made a name for myself, by breaking the rules. Some guard looked the other way when a rule was broken. As long as their supervisors didn't know about it. If our cell wasn't inspection ready they gave you a chance to straighten it out. 12s took pleasure in writing you up. In my former years I didn't give a damn about being wrote up. Their intimidations didn't work for me. I remember times on a bad day. Everybody had those moments where they just didn't care about nothing. I didn't feel like getting my cell ready for inspection. Inspection was from 9:30 am – 4:30 pm. All your property had to be placed in a wall locker according to a diagram. Your bed had to be made up military style. Your shoes had to be aligned under the bunk. And the cell had to be in sanitary condition, no dust. So I stayed in bed that morning up til inspection. Even though breaking that rule meant 14 days in the hole along with a write up. Most guys preferred doing time on lock up just to avoid the morning inspections.

It wasn't being incarcerated. I was learning more about my new identity trying to apply those concepts in a world that despise me. Was the issue for me. It felt like I was fighting two wars. Self forgiveness help me see that getting to know my purpose in life. And my place in it. Didn't involve my punishment. Two years was enough for me to realize. I needed a change. Quite naturally I was dealing with some anger as well. I mean I left behind a family. What man doesn't suffer behind those he have left behind. My only son not having a father to raise and take care of him. I wanted for D.J. What I had at some point. And even more upon growing into his manhood. Thus, I failed him. I remember moments of pure peer pressure. Trying so hard to remove such pain, but you can't. How to fix this problem without doing it the wrong way? And to be honest. At times I allowed my anger to control me. Not caring about how such behavior will only make things worse. If you ever been in my shoes. Then you know exactly where I'm going. Leaving your child behind to face the real world. Can make you or break you. Fortunately, there were moments in visitation. I did feel more of a father during those two hours of visiting D.J. Over coming such hurdles can be a means to be a better person. I know it's easier said than done. But believe me, it was a real test. And I welcomed it. I recall a brother Malik who I looked up to. He was our prayer leader and very knowledgeable. I would meet him on the yard every morning on wellness walk. We would talk for hours about certain struggles, making sacrifices for God. Malik was good at interpreting the text, applying such revelation to our own life experience even here in prison. Most of those stories helped me solve my issues. He told me inspiration is a means to build inner coping strategies to fight off evil. And the biggest fight is yourself, he reminded me. The more I thought about that, the more sense it made. The more I reflected. The better I felt within. I began to see how my situation was shaping my spiritual self. I no longer allowed those things to hinder me. Instead I used them as lessons, just something in life being tested.

... ...

2012 is the year I became open about my sexuality. I was tired of hiding that secret also. I'll admit it was rough at first. Not being accepted among so many anti homophobic people. I had to denounce my religious lifestyle because being a queer man was forbidden. But that didn't change my spiritual self. From the inside and out side of prison. I developed close ties with my new community. This help me transition into the community. I did more socializing with those who shared similar experiences, while giving me the support I needed. I was at Calhoun State Prison. It was my first medium security prison. Here the population was a lot calmer compared to close security prisons where I spent 10 years. Although my members and I were a minority group. People were more friendly. And more respected. I was shocked to see members having positions in different working areas. Which made it a lot better getting the things I needed. I wasn't naive about being who I am. So I kept my guards up at all times. Every now and then. I would get into a heated argument just to prove I got balls. I have always been a calmer person. I don't ever remember getting into a fist fight at Calhoun. What I don't like is people who are the opposite, being somebody their not. In brief self forgiveness involves a turning point. Doing work internally and removing such guilt or shame. Any other feelings isn't you. I figured just as the inner self needed some work, the outer self also. I tell people all the time. The best feeling in the world is living your life. I truly believe the soul is our core, so lead with your heart. No matter what.

There were so many lessons. I can point out. When we successfully reach that comfort zone in life. Such faith I believe is associated with acknowledging the truth. Taking responsibility for what you have done. And learning from those experiences which gave reasoning to act alone. Becomes the truth for feeling guilty. Not long after my father passed away. I discovered a simple way to resolve the guilt I felt. Although I wasn't face to face saying, I'm sorry for all the disappointment getting in trouble and coming back to prison. Just that confession alone was enough for me. It was closing the door behind me. I chose a quiet time in my cell at night. Alone in total darkness. I'm relaxed and focused with a clear head. While my father is setting across from me. Just like in our last visit two years ago at Waycross. His handsome smile. I'm remorse sharing my confession. All the feelings between us is a reminder just how special this moment means to me. What was hidden is now a open chapter in my life. Dad's solemn advise, Son just keep doing what you doing. You will make it.

CHAPTER 23

That was the reassurance I needed. Dad was talking about the spiritual in me that was keeping me alive. So I continued setting out that purpose. And doing what I felt was natural. This didn't happen by surprise, but the fact I wanted it. Not like any desires we just purchase to satisfy our pleasure. No that joy ride was over. I considered making the choices I felt right for me regardless how others may feel. A majority of the prison population consist of gang bangers. This group is highly noticed, and have a huge following among young brothers coming to prison.

Now back in 2000. If you was gang banging it wasn't notice unless the person was asked Who are you? Today, you don't have to ask because they like to flag their gang color. If you are a Blood your flag was red. If you was a Crip the flag was blue. I notice how divided the groups are and very territorial. They mostly kept to themselves in prison. And was quick to let you know who was running the show in the units. I have witness more gang wars than I can count. I remember, during my time at Waycross 2010. There was a gang war between the gangs and Mexicans that year. A lot of people died that day too. I stayed as far away as possible by locking down in my cell. It became a routine whenever something popped off. And fortunately for me I had never been involved in a gang war, even during my affiliation with the religious group. As far as I can remember. I never met or knew any gang bangers growing up. Matter, fact the first time was during my time at Valdosta State Prison. I was almost 3 months away from maxing out my bid. I was in a program called ITP, used for breaking inmates. It was ran like a boot camp, but with strict rules. We eat, dressed, marched, and trained like real soldiers in the military. I hated it like hell. Frog was a blood. He was my neighbor living next to my cell. We both were from Atlanta so we became tight during our bid.

Although I never understood why someone would prefer gang banging. I don't view them any differently than the thug life style I once lived. The next time I ran into Frog. I was working at Kroger's as a stock clerk on the night shift. To much surprise. Frog had his own tattoo parlor in the same neighborhood I worked.

Unfortunately, I did notice the connection with a limited belief system. Which tells me the proper way of living nonspiritual has yet to be defined. History tell us. During the 1930s the new prison idea became known as the Rehabilitation model of corrections. According to this idea. The social intellectual or biological deficiencies of criminals were the cause of their crimes. Also named the Medical Model, however not in my opinion. That is just like saying all men are born equal. But that's man limited understanding versus the natural laws of mankind. This is not a process that we can use in any system. Nor apply for the good we see in every day life. Thus, we become divided in our unconscious thinking that idea is possible no matter what. Which reminds me what mama use to say, You just like your dad. However the case. I believe our own spiritual should lead the way. Allowing that core self to be our vessel in any situation we may encounter in life.

They say 90 days is the future. Beyond that is non existent. For example, my parole month is coming up in three months. Now the thought. I might not make it, is my limited understanding oppose to the truth. I will not get out of prison thinking that way. Not the way to change any situation. I have to spend time working on the future. A few years ago. I did some research on how to better manage my small business career goals. I spent the most part looking at scanty books in the prison library. I found one book that interest me. I have a bad habit not returning books on time. Not every book can be read three days. So, instead I cuffed the book inside a folder while signing out at the front counter. Depending on the subject I'd keep the book for months. Before returning it back to the library. And this was such a book. The unknown author was an American pupil in Europe majoring in business and marketing. Later advancing his education in Japan. Single handily taking the task. Learning the skills takes time but less cost. Instead of me paying a tuition at a school. I saved a lot of money learning it on my own. Even though such references were limited. I gathered what little I could from the library and got down to business.

Spending hours of researching studying was fun. I quickly devised a plan having a limited amount of resources. I couldn't give up. So I did what was natural living off the land. A slang word we use in prison. Equivalent to a street hustle. And since I was already working in the food service, kitchen. I took what I could and sold the food to the general population. Hustling out the kitchen also provided a way for basic needs plus books to further my education. Sometimes I'd except contraband from my customers depending on what it was. Then turn around and sale it. Cutting them off meant lesser money. Another hustle was trafficking things for brothers. Because most of them didn't have the privilege of getting out side the dorms. Whatever they had to relocate, I made sure it got there.

CHAPTER 24

This was during the time I met Willy. Him and I developed a friendship before he made parole 2013. He was from Athens Georgia. A small town where not much happened. Although I haven't heard from him in a long time. I was surprised he kept his word staying in touch. I was no longer living a religious lifestyle, yet I wasn't aware that a person doesn't have to be religious in order to be deeply spiritual. This feeling felt more of a relief. Not like my former experience. Similar picture like the characters on O.Z. No heart, No love, No home, just stripped from everything. I didn't feel alone anymore. But I was missing a shadow. Someone to bond with in the hopes of being long term friends. And building a better life in prison. I guess that's the down side. Because when Willy left I had no one to replace him. It seems like every time I get attach to someone. I get disappointed later because the system is designed that way. It will eventually separate you from what is natural. So how was it possible, in a world with so much hate for being the man I am? This kind of social injustice I didn't like on certain levels.

The answers to such thoughts. Came much sooner. It was a week before New Year's 2013. I transferred to Washington State Prison that summer. I was currently in segregation for refusing housing in the general population. I had just gotten an unexpected letter from a old friend. Jamie Hurston and I had met through my cell mate years ago, 2003. I notice the familiar address written on the envelope. And the same fragrance perfume. I couldn't believe it. Why. I didn't know what to think of this. Her and I had been the best of friends. This was before we broke up seven years ago. She broke things off due to being in love with someone else. The separation was disappointing for me. I held back a lot of emotions. I didn't want to look weak like other dudes in here when their girlfriends jump ship. I promise myself it'll never be me. Yet, at the same time I felt betrayed also. But, I learned to move on. I figured if I can recover from the lost of a family.

Then I could get through this as well. Who am I to blame her for such suffering? I brought this on myself. Only a selfish person can't keep it real. A person who hasn't accepted responsibility, is only concern about themselves. Keeping it real hasn't always been the case but I'm learning to consider the next person. You must be real with your self before anyone else can see the real in you. Now, as I look back. I see a pattern. As I'm reading her letter, the words, Please forgive me. I was wrong for what I done to you, Derrick. Was written more times than I can count. That message stood out. I needed to hear and feel those words because it reminded me of how I viewed my own self forgiveness. It felt strange. I never looked at it like this. No one has never confess to me like this before. Such thoughts like, Was she playing with my head? Was she just trying to use me? I started to doubt her letter. She was more than sorry.

Then there were some misconceptions also. I had to be honest. So I wrote Jamie back. I wanted to know more about the time we spent apart. Who was she dating? Where was the letters I wrote? Do you still love him? I needed confirmation because I didn't want to be pulled back into the same deception a second time. Then looking at my current status. I figured no way. I was about to continue on this way, alone. And, found every excuse to forgive her, which made perfect sense. Given the chance for this opportunity felt good. And bad at the same time. Thinking from two distinct places based on different principles. Often times is difficult for me explaining how prison works. Women lead with their emotions. So I had to be careful sharing such experiences here in prison. It's never been easy. I came to realize it would confuse the situation more than it already was. Maybe not the right time. And some things are better left untold. I never remember being so judge mental until now. I guess it was due to me. Making some adjustments editing people and returning back to the general population. After getting Jamie's letter I decided that the change was for the better. Cutting ties with people wasn't so easy, but I had no other choices. Because my normal involvement with prison life. I believe was creating inner conflicts with those I assume was my friend's. People I thought I could trust. Although, suddenly their energy had changed. And the more I tried to ignore the signs. The more personal it felt pulling me away from positivity.

Such bad company. Only incurred immaturity with those I took as friends. No wonder why I felt alone. Yet it didn't seem to effect me from being myself. Who was I really? What have I learned from the past? Where am I going? Not only did I choose to do the right thing. But I made a promise, that nothing is going to stop me for doing it.

However, I remained focused on the bigger picture. This was my fight. No more living in denial as a distraction. I'm tired of the insecurity and loneliness.

My need and desires for loving myself. Will continue being directed at the heart of those who believe in me. And as I gradually took a glance back. Such memories were just mere acts. Always loosing a battle with self and co-depending on others to resolve the damage inside me. Why, desire attention only to abuse it later? My close relationships weren't always the same. I realize that there were factors. Towards understanding the real issue between them. From a realistic view. All partners in some way co-depend on each other. Not the other way around.

No matter how often the abuse he / she acts towards you. It's a false invention motivated by a suffering heart. You may not heed the signs because there is no genuine love given back. Like the saying, What you put in it. Is what you get out of it. The results usually happens in a failing relationship both needs not being met, left unfulfilled. Similar, both partners at times.

May act out mean motivated due to neglecting one another attention and communication. This a common in relationships. Why he didn't answer my text or call? What is wrong with her? Such negative self talk can play out, triggering the behavior adding more suffering than anything.

CHAPTER 25

Never think your age. Can determine how well you understand the world as an adult. We naturally acquire knowledge through storing information in our mind. Thus rather we choose to act upon it depends on several factors. Most young brothers in particular often commit crimes impulsively but can change over the course of decades in prison. My problem was being influenced by others. When I think about it. Such memories reminds me how my former life took so many years to learn. What I found. Was the same thing that brought me to Identifying my true self. This reconnection felt so familiar. As if the person inside never left me. As self guilt shook my very soul. It hadn't occurred to me that our King David went through a similar experience. Because the more he sought in judgement and executions over the common people throughout Israel and Egypt. The more injustice he committed. His God still forgave his sins. His concubines appetite led to his down fall. Yet he was a man of God calling upon Him in fervent prayer.

The story of Sampson gives us an example also. What can be the results when we lack commitment in God. Seeking self dependency outside Godly substance. Or when our hearts are inclined to the things of the world. Like Sampson was favored as a Nazirate one who is appointed to be faithful to God. Our personal relationship with

God. Comes before anything even our family let alone the partners we love. Our communion with Him is essential in all intimate relationships, especially marriage. But sometimes these commitments fail. For obvious reasons not known to us. Just as Eve was easily tricked by the devil. Causing both partners to sin because they didn't follow instructions. For the most part having a mature nature becomes less of a burden. By the ungodly things in our world. That's the importance of not allowing your mind to be manipulated and deceived by the world. And always keep in mind. We are who we think. I try to keep the world separate from the spiritual thinking, especially when I'm being tested. Reading spiritual literature along with the Bible. Will help you get a better understanding, also. Author's like James P. Gill. There are many lessons to learn in his books, like Moses struggles in becoming a mature leader. It takes a lot of work and time becoming a man of God. The choices are your own. We must look at our circumstances the way it is until the calling directs us to change course. A lot of times. We are gifted with things but use them the wrong way. We hold a certain status thinking we are better than those who are less fortunate. Or thinking we know it all. The opposite is walking in faith not by sight. Seeking the pleasure and selfish motives of the world.

My mental health counselor Williams. Comes to my cell every week. During her visits she always give me a chart with different advice about our thoughts. How to find happiness? This is not about just being grateful for stuff, but for the simple things of life. If things are not going as well as you like. Find the silver lining in the cloud and be thankful for it. And if you are on top of the world, celebrate at those moments. Your change probably want happen over night, next month or a year from now. But gradually a change man will eventually become a reality you can appreciate. A man who join what is good. And forbid what is wrong. Men that honor their parents leading by example. Even if you fail to yield spiritually. It's still not over with yet, because we are all prone to do wrong. But we can get back up too. Fortunately, for me. Looking at such experiences right here in prison points to many ups and downs. Man I'm blessed. Because things could've been a lot worse. Having someone in my corner, sharing this life with me. Is a great feeling.

CHAPTER 26

Upon my renewing and healing. The changes provided some answers to some deeply rooted spirituality. I was taught from a religious view more than a spiritual life in prison ministry. Although, at the time such views did nourish a healthy spiritual life. Like God is one, prayer, fasting, are required in most organized religions. And almost every religious teaching will tell you. That the purpose of life on earth is to maintain union with your true nature. Do I have to wear a head covering? Should I attend morning worship every Sunday? Can I eat pork? My past experiences with religion was exclusive. I didn't believe in it's principal's. Which diluted and twisted my life. It also caused internal strive within the community. A person will say. I know what the law said, but we are in prison. But yet I thought the spiritual was inclusive. It is unchangeable no matter if you are living in Alaska 180 degrees below zero. We all supposed to be sub servant to the spiritual. I remember awhile ago. At this medium security prison where I had two roommate's. The one who was Christian. He kept his Bible on the wall table. I notice whenever I'd ask to use it he'd make up some lame excuses denying me. So about three weeks later. The other roommate moves in who also happens to be a Christian. I was coming off the yard from a long work out. Upon entering the cell my plan was to take a shower. Then get on the phone to call my mom.

A routine I had developed over the years. The Bible owner was setting on my bed but quickly stood up with blank a expression. I just held my tongue, getting my things for the shower and left the room. Like nothing happened.

You will find a lot of repeated offender's join religion in prison. Only to leave it behind when they get released. I don't know if this is a sign, causing them to return back to prison. But we call it Jail house religion. We all can use deeper rooted spirituality to grow. But everyone don't want it. I never had a hard time comprehending and applying knowledge because for one. I sure had more than enough time to study. How we can not grow spiritual? Perhaps my failure owning up to such concepts confused me. I always felt naturally free inside. Which can be a major hurdle growing more religiously in relation to behavior and faith. Any tenant involving the theory that every man as a result of his failure. Can not continue in the good, except by the constant assistant of worshipping the divine. Is on the right track I believe. A man can become egotistically free from natural limitations just by living morally wrong rejecting the divine. Is the very opposite. However, such a person may not know how to worship God. I guess what keeps me balance is the fact believing in a God. And when a man reach a level of spirituality he acts on knowledge. Along with his natural inclinations to behave in only what is good. Such is the case, any learned behavior that influenced a person to commit a crime. Similar process but with a set of different rules, thus resulting in a indeterminate punishment. The very first response is fear. How long will I be behind these walls? That becomes our focus unconsciously not considering our behavior towards those we afflicted pain upon. And, think we can still win the fight. When in fact, we fail ourselves by choosing a belief system that's impossible to sustain us.

... ...

One day I asked a ex-gang member. After, noticing other roommates act out the same behavior from the same affiliation group. Why do GDs like to keep the cell dark all day? His response was that those brothers have a dark side. Which describes their mood of discontentment, misery, and frustration being in prison. I tried to make sense of that metaphor but came empty of reason. I did discern such behavior is definitely abnormal. Compared to a brother like myself who need light to read. I'll be the first to admit prison can steal your dignity. Even those who appear tough, on the out side. While the inside is weak and heartless. At one point that was me. And most of us are aware of such inner struggles. We just to stubborn to choose other alternatives that will solve our problems. Trust me. You don't want a life sentence here in prison. That's a kind of suffering hard to come to grips with. I'm talking about a real bad degenerate place. Such problems will make you wonder, Why do God put me through this? Do He know what is happening to me? If, He knows and loves me then, Why isn't He answering my prayers? Truth be told. We can also suffer from doing right. If we look closer. It's clear our beliefs in good and bad of the world is ruled by our creator. This is called a divine preordainment. Who has already decided in all matters, which can be difficult to process.

Biblical history claims at the beginning. The world was destroyed because the evil of mankind was extremely great on earth. And every intention man thought from his soul was only evil without limit. Just consider this for a moment. Today our world may not compare to the ills of our primitive times. But we are not far behind. Fortunately, for some brothers behind the wall would, rather use divine intervention towards living a meaningful life. I remember being in a study class. The lecture was on the subject of behavior and manners according to the divine book. The instructor asked, If we was to loose all of our assets, What will be the only thing we have left? After a roar of failing answers from the class. I waited until the room calmed down and said. Good behavior and manners. And although that lesson took place over fifteen years ago. I still follow that example from a wise scholar. Before I continue on to the next chapter. I also want to point out that identifying with your spirituality is an inclusive part of being natural. Whether you are guided by divine intervention, or not. It's immoral thinking we don't need love, compassion, and courage.

That's crazy.

CHAPTER 27

I still remember the first time Mama and Gloria seen my girlfriend Jamie. It happened so suddenly during the fall of 2018. I do remember the introduction through conversations on the phone, but never knew how the connections all started. I guess I never paid close attention. Or I simply didn't know them as well as I thought. So anyways I ask Mama to do me a favor. Instead of Jamie going over mama house to pick up my request, mama decided against it. Why don't I just drop it off at his place. She never uses the correct pronouns. Never. Although I'm quick to remind her that Jamie is a transgender, so please respect her identity. Over looking someone's ignorance is necessary in most cases. But sometimes I feel it's intended out of self respect too. The following day I believe mama pulls up in her driveway. Just setting in her car waiting on Jamie to come out the house. Well in my opinion mama just wanted to see for her self. A person curiosity works in many ways. Meeting them in person makes the assessment more better. It allows them to better understand the person's behavior and character. So, this meeting for the first time gave meaning to so many thoughts. I always viewed it as a way of Mama's condition of supporting her son. I don't know the words to define their connection, however I can say they became friends. And sometimes their chemistry makes me feel jealous. And they know just the time to turn against me in a dual disagreement.

Mama never shared her personal views about Jamie. I thought it was strange. Why wouldn't a parent be curious about her sons lover? Or What the future holds between the two of them? Well I do know they shared a value that was connected to me. And, obviously at some point there must have been a mention about me in private. All women talk. However, I know there were inquiries about my mama, I do recall. Do you think your Mama will accept us together? Jamie would ask me about certain things I wasn't quite sure about either. I never really cared. I always felt that our relationship was separate from family. Or anyone for that matter. Our thoughts and beliefs are independent from such people who may view things differently. But never the same. I simply explained that all relationships hold value that is determined how much work is involved between them. Those values must be genuine. Just the fact being conceived into the world by loving parents. Don't mean the child will grow up, equivocally as them. Which I explained, this staging process in my former chapter's. In retrospect, my youth VS. the life I chose for myself in some ways never effected the conditional love both parents continued to give me. Although I made it difficult at times. However, nothing stood in my way for making such choices. Being separated from mama over a long period of time. Revealed so many unanswered questions for me. And as this growing mature man took root. I sought out to understand

Why such lessons seem to have a connection to my childhood. Now I know. Mama knew I was a mild little child. I stayed mostly to myself. I was picked on because I wasn't brave enough. I would easily cry out of emotions. She had to see the signs.

Then as time past on. I began to build courage towards facing my enemies and behaving in ways I wasn't taught by my parents. A sudden change took over me. And secretly mama continue hoping that I would turn out to become the man she'd be proud one day soon. She held back. Never shared that thought with me. But was quick to remind me saying, You just like your dad. Never living up to mama expectations. And while trying to define that man on my own. I was met with a familiar past. I believe this was normal for most brothers in my city. Especially, for the parents, a social illness that has given birth to a over crowding prison system. No parent seemed to know the correct way of living as a family. And for that reason. Mama still have unresolved and hidden hurt from long ago.

Just the other week. Jamie drove my mama and Gloria down to visit me. The visit to Valdosta was supposed to be a surprise for my birthday. But I was secretly informed by my girlfriend before they showed up. I couldn't wait to inquire about my son DJ current status. How is he doing these days? He was still living with my mama in which I was thankful. Before then he was living with his aunt Kara, but that didn't work out to good. And before that he was sharing an apartment with a friend on the West side. That reminded me how I use to switch up place to place. Mama wouldn't give me the details, she never do. Why you don't ask DJ? I guess this was her way of protecting his privacy. I took a long look at mama setting across from me. And although I'm not certain what I read. But I felt her pain. Then I took in Gloria's calm bleak face. She is looking in the other direction. Gloria is the youngest of her two siblings. Her short frail frame is motionless. She is undaunted by a stroke and diabetes. I'm still amazed at her strength each day. Although she died months later. Just as I imitate her stare in the direction of the visitor's next to us. She gives me this disturbing look. And instantly she makes a childish like smirk. Then we all burst into laughing.

CHAPTER 28

My girlfriend is full of surprises. You can bet. She is going to remind her man when his birthday has arrived. And it's a different card all the time. This year it was a little boy and girl image on the front cover. With the images standing side by side holding hands. Last year a woman and man kissing. And the year before that a teenage girl and boy. I think the average of incoming letter's I received each week is three. So you can imagine what my cell smells like during mail call. It breaks my heart when the staff do a routine shake down. Like I said, depending on the person. Some guards don't take there job seriously caring out unnecessary punishment. We are aloud a limit of twenty letters. Anything over that is considered contraband and they give you two options, send it back or destroy it. Well in most cases. I'll just send my letters back to Jamie because destroying them wasn't a option period. I don't remember, it happening but once or twice. But despite any given situation, we always kept close ties. Which is the reason our friendship has grown stronger. Tell me why life be full of surprises also? Well I had some terrible news not long after my birthday. I just so happen to call Jamie one morning around 9am. I learned that her house had caught on fire just moment's ago. About 65% of the house was burned to the ground. Fortunately, she had survived the incident, caused by a broken floor heater. All she remember, was waking up coughing in a cloud of black smoke. And running in the dark towards the exit door. As I listen, I hear a man asking her questions.

Jamie is breathing heavy choosing her words carefully. Some things she don't remember. It's in the house she said, to the man in the back ground. I'm picturing a man taking notes on his writing tablet. I wait wanting to aid her but there is nothing I can do at the moment. I hear the loud voices and sirens in the distance. The whole neighborhood seem to have came alive all suddenly. I wait still. Yeah, baby! Who was that I ask? Hoping whatever the guy is looking for is found inside the house. All I could do was listen as she told me the details. She grew more upset it seems at her self. She was crying and being apologetic towards her own insecurities. I couldn't believe what I was hearing, the fact that she could've died. I had discovered that the fire destroyed most of the master bedroom. Her room. As she was telling me about all the valuables destroyed. I thought about the painting I drew for her birthday. It was a huge eagle over looking a forest in the back ground. I was glad to hear it had survived also. Most of her personal needs were gone. And in the center of the bedroom ceiling lay a massive hole. I vision men aiming a water hose from the yard, while the water trickle down into the hole putting out the fire. What the fire didn't destroy the water defiled. Outside, a crowd of on lookers gather watching the scene. My girlfriend is still upset. She is worried about how her mother is going to take the bad news. Her house. Along with the fact, she was raised in this house. I can imagine the emotions she was feeling at the moment. I can relate. Thinking back at my own childhood memories. She felt so alone. However, she had already broken the news to her two sisters and some friends. Jude was her friend I didn't like. So during that phone call. Jude just happen to show up. Her only concern is her deserted dog that ran away two weeks ago. Bitch, my house is on fire, Jamie yelled. You should've came and got him when I called you. I haven't seen your dog.

That particular friend has a habit of using my girlfriend. And normally she allows her since it's hard for her to just say no. They'd been friends a long time ago before Jamie and I met. Time after time. I always reminded her that Jude is a self centered person who is only out for self, nothing else. And if she continues being kind to her, she's going to regret it soon. I guess what seemed like a decade of preaching, she finally threw in the towel. Before this, my girlfriend let Jude move in. Just imagine taking in two adults, two kids, and a dog rent free. Well, it was supposed to be a payment every month. But, that promise was a big lie. So the little lies started each month like I'm looking for a job. I recall reading her letters talking about this no good friend. They eating all my food. They want get a job. They want clean up the dog shit. Hell, that's what you get for not listening to me! Sometimes I'd just listen at her complain on the phone. How they all stressing her out every day.

At the conclusion, the house wasn't completely demolished. But not livable either. So, Jamie needed a place to stay, plus shelter for her two dogs. Fortunately, her close cousin took her inn along with Sadie's. Sadie's is her house dog. Angle was a mix bull dog which was left at the house to guard it. I thought it was a better idea asking my mama who lived alone and could use some help around the house. Jamie also, could've moved back into her house on the Westside. Which, she was renting it to a friend, and needed the money. Come to find out. This friend that's living their was two months behind her rent, which I thought was crazy. That was a constant issue with my girlfriend keeping bad company with people just out to use her. After about three months. While the house was being restored by some building contractors in the Atlanta area. The first burglary occurred one night, but nothing of real value was taken. Now after living with her cousin five months, she wants her own place. We all are waiting. Especially, after discovering that the contractor's have delayed their promise to be finished with the house. I was hoping before my parole month. But with her weekly check ups don't look like that's going to happen. A good residential plan is a must for parole. Having a strong support from your community or family is important as well. So I reminded myself to do a update just in case. I received an email the other day from DJ. The message was longer than normal he seemed excited. And the words were from a much older young man. I knew it took courage as I read his letter. That hit me deep. Thought's of a youthful boy growing up apart from his father. No role model. Yet, still I'm very proud he didn't choose the path his father took. He took the time showing concern and support. I recall DJ saying, I hope to see you real soon. Not the former visits we use to have here in prison. But, meeting face to face in the real world. Because there was a lot of things he wanted to know about me. I quickly wiped a running tear. I responded with a email, attached an e- card to my son. It's been a month since that occurred. Such moments don't happen often as I like but I'm thankful it finally did. Was it a mere coincidence my son living with mama? I had so many mix emotions about his present situation.

CHAPTER 29

I hold no judgement against these unexpected conflicts. I have had my share of problems and don't see justice in creating problems for others. So I'm always reminded how both worlds have an abundance of problems for everyone living anywhere. It makes no difference what back ground a person has had. Their highest grade level. Or a variety of difference that prove us to be all apart of humanity. In the past year, such violence, assaults, and deaths has been the case on the Tier Program. The other day there was an incident. As I looked out the tray flap. A young man decided to toss a cup of feces at me. Then yelled all types of cuss words. I became so angry that I found myself ready to do battle. But I thought better. And the response wasn't what everyone expected because the dorm had calmed down. Everyone thought I was going to retaliate against him. Not even some obscenities back at him or tossing some two week old urine at him. Instead, I ducked my head back inside and closed the tray flap avoiding the circus. By doing so I killed their fun. I just set there in deep thoughts for a moment, not giving into my bruise ego. My fist intuition was to fight back. I was going to throw a bottle of old urine at him. I could never play in shit, under no circumstances. However, I took control thinking before making a foolish mistake. It was just a tear. Something way to familiar, looking back at my experience here among these brothers.

It kind of remind me. How the bullies at school use to act towards me. Only, now I've taken down those walls, allowing myself to be humble and strong. A person comfortable with who they are. And their place in the world. Have defined peace. We give situations the meaning in our lives. We men have to lead by example. By making choices for the better good. Then acting on such decisions that will make us successful. And even, if our ego is put to the test, which seems almost impossible to control at times. It would rather be in the best interest for us to walk away from such conflicts altogether. Because always remember, that our choice is our understanding, what we decide is the outcome of that choice we made for ourselves. And how we see people and circumstances has a lot to do with the way we feel. Here is another eye opener. You think your situation is difficult, creating all kinds of conflicts. Try trading places with me. And I bet you. Prison will be the most trouble some, and unethical place you've ever wanted to live. All prison's are inhumane designed to limit people from their fullest potential. They all have such inability to operate and function as a vehicle that inspires men to be mentally and physically free. And as a result. We rather continue the path set out for ourselves after committing such crime and being sentence a life in prison. I can't relate to a man who can not show responsibility. Then to make matters worse they allow the system to make choices for them. A system created to demoralize

you. What sane individual prefer this life over the real society? Look at the bigger picture. I don't judge those brothers because we are all prone for failure. I understand their shallow out look about life. Or such limited believe system. I mean there are times I get pulled into the mist things from time to time.

... ...

When it comes to equal rights among a group living together here in prison. I think about our vast social system world wide. We are no different now, than we were back then. As time swiftly move into the present world. History continue to be a repetitive cycle. Such progressive system had a tremendous impact for the African Americans life post medieval England, Africa, and the United States. These countries introduced the hallmark of human bondage we still see today. It points out the ugly mask our law makers and politicians try so hard to ignore. But, unfortunately time has proven over many times that you can not close out the world. Not never. Upon attaining any rights, we must first understand it from a judicial process decided by people of a higher authority. Then such law ratified becomes abiding upon the people living in such society. So, in contrast let's look at our primitive era. Let's try understanding how or what ethical meant living in bondage. This starts at the medieval period A.D 4761450 West Africa and Europe.

Long before the explorer Columbus discovered land in ancient America. West Africa among other people had already made contact with Native Americans. In fact, before the Europeans conqueror's invaded Africa carrying away people. Human slavery was being practiced in the West Africa. Surprisingly against their own but it was not the form of bondage the Europeans developed force labor. A slave was allowed to keep their rights for example, a person could own property, get involved in judicial processes, own a slave, inter marry with kin, and be a beneficiary of the slave owner. Tribalism has been their tradition for ages. It was apartheid that had adulterated the African and trade routes along the Black Sea. As it was in England the defeated were required to pledge obedience to the winner and to meet obligations. The P.O.W's was taught to honor their owners but kept their personal identity. Similar to South Africans subjugation of villages by enslaving the leaders. For this reason. African Americans has long suffered a more harsh form of slavery. And yet still after it's establishment in the 1600. America remains the highest rates of incarceration in the world. In addition the most populated in jails and prisons are blacks. Unfortunately, for this awareness was the cornerstone of a new perception of myself, and other's living in prison. In light of the world view on civil rights and social equality. Everywhere I'm met with differences that makes me a human. And, here is this group saying to me. We don't think it's okay. I took a considerable amount of time reeducating myself. In finding out, Why so many efforts had been rejected by the Negro problem. I had this hunger like many reform prisoners discovering their true identity. Where my roots first began in order to understand Who I am.

Prison has a dynamic affect on a person. Especially, serving a long sentence which means more time. So that gave me more time than I needed reading the books. I had to reject the believes and traditions of my parents. It was a hard thing to do. Such concepts of the new Christianity had long ago distorted my ancestors tradition. While I later struggle to be a practical Muslim, but that idea was obviously adulterated by false teachings. I witness how prison use religion to justify mistreatment, segregation, and privilege to render inmates sub servant to obedience. Naturally, I understand that I'm a normal human. With my own identity. To see myself an achiever of any man regardless of race, sex, or culture. Inwardly I see nothing I don't understand. And again I spend a lot of time looking inside myself. I try very hard some nights. Immersing my thoughts about the present future. For example, some people will never understand. Because it's not meant for them to know, either they refuse to learn. Certain knowledge don't profit them. Or, they're not interested in learning. So, what else should that world have involved? Having to grow up here in prison. Becoming my own man. I believe held the truth to the answers I was determined to find out the whole story.

Some people just to blind to see. What struck me. Was that the negro went through great lengths towards equality. Mainly race making slow progress than it should've been.

Growing increasingly impatient with the oppressor and pace to change their circumstances. I honestly believe that the problem wasn't the conflict of mixing the black and white. Neither an independent group in the broader struggle to join the forces that be in politics, economics, and culture. No matter who is setting on the thrown or strategy used. The problem facing the negro lies within his very soul, he can not remember his beginning. The father the negro gets from his historical pioneers. In the present America. The more he lack to know and understand his African heritage. It just doesn't make sense screaming black power at any cost. Without having first. A clear consciousness of the purpose intended as a group.

CHAPTER 30

The last founder of a great leader Malcolm X understood. But did his followers really understand the man directive actions or objections? Why he made a transition as he did? Similar to my own experience getting a more deeper educated look.

I also believe that all humans have limited rights but not equal. It would be unmanageable for me thinking that everybody. Is capable of doing the task better than me. Or perhaps write a book as good. Mama always reminded me that Michelle and I could attain the same grade. But had an unequal level of understanding life all together. No matter our age, gender, or test score. There is this unique natural process inside that sets us apart from one another. I gradually understood the difference between us. I began to realize how affective this process is in my present situation. We are all victims in many ways. We're victims of false imprisonment, exploitation, injustice etc. And as a consequence designed to further keep us in bondage. We are stripped of dignity and stricken with rules to guarantee a false sense of belonging. But as often enough we loath our inhumane conditions tempered by feelings of insecurity and fear. The high spirits to control self becomes intolerable so we act out. And it's okay. We in a sense are naturally untamed. We loose control unconsciously because we have no control in changing our present situation.

We make every excuse. Blame other's only to create far reaching problems that we might not be able to change later. In retrospect, we act without knowing why. We go against our natural inclinations. Thus, the outcome will always be failure. And the reason we repeated history. With that reality. We must know the difference like a tree can not with stand without a strong foundation to uphold it. No matter how many seasons it has survived lacking proper nourishment from the sun and rain. Will make it weak. So it remains unstable. Let's look at it this way. And I have to keep it real. Being victimized for who you are some times is just a part of being human, although it isn't fare to anyone. I never cared about how someone felt towards me. We can not totally please everyone we meet. That's just something we have to accept and keep it moving. Or better yet, check it or respect it. Is usually my response to kill the rhetoric intended towards me. You for whatever reason. May be a in a gang but you don't bang in their hood, so you get shot at. You is innocent but they said you raped a woman. You may be white but you called a black man a nigger, and so on. We give situations the meaning they have in our lives. And we can choose either way. Such choices become my own thoughts and decisions to make. No one is entitled to make that choice for me. For me it took many years to change the view of the world. It occurred to me that this whole process is based on how I identify myself. Oppose to the natural order of prison life. What I found were a complex of issues. Mainly the good vs. bad that exit within me. Which will always be at odds with the natural no matter how I see myself in it.

I recently found out through a phone call. That the parole board denied my release. I was very disappointed and upset at the news. Just that quick I wanted to give up. Their reason after a review of my case: Is insufficient amount of time served to date given the nature and circumstances of your offences. I was going to give them a reason. Beyond the decision that had already been made. I couldn't believe this shit. I thought about the possibility of being placed in the Tier segregation unit here at Valdosta. Did this have anything to do with them denying me? Not, necessarily so, because they would have said something like. Given the facts of your current situation, we the board deny you parole. However, I was set off for my next review in 2023. I remember reading their policy about the reviewing process. That the board may reconsider changing a prior decision in a case for any reason. At any time up to the time of release. Of course I had been disappointed at my own actions for being on the Tier program. That assignment alone may or might not have persuade the board's decision. I don't know. But, I had to accept it and move on towards coping with my present situation. From experience I've learned that mentally bondage when use effectively can be very powerful for changing conditions. It's a lesson I've learned over the years. No matter if you are the victim of being punished. It shouldn't prevent you from making progress.

CHAPTER 31

Now when I'm met with such emotional stigma. Normally I think first before reacting subconsciously. Because 99% of the time. I have encountered that very same experience in the past. No doubt it's easier said than done. But it's doable if you are sincere. Although, prison is a very complicated system to understand living morally right. Do what you can do. To the best of your ability while focusing long and hard. Once you have done what you intend preferably with the pen. The next step is with the heart and soul. Not always easy to accept living around so much negativity. Making you feel even more boxed in than you actually are. Just because I didn't receive a fair trail to prove my innocence. Don't mean I have to live in prison day after day with a victim mentality. Another thing I do. And the most effective method is training the mind using simple skills like reading, writing, and exercises. To help flush out being lazy or idling time doing foolish things. Both working the mind and body muscles is good, especially isolated in a cell alone. I made sure the course is divided into three parts. For example, I chose two hours of yoga, pacing the cell, and stretching before and after the work out. And at noon 3-4 hours left reading and writing. Then for the evening I might select some down time listening to the radio. I recall writing my girlfriend last night. In the letter I made a joke about her age. She just turned 56 a few days ago. Every since the day we met she always had a age complex, never admitting her true age. So, why celebrate a birthday? She loves my greeting cards I drew and mailed to her. This year I designed using this old one I restored. The inside was fashioned with her lipstick prints.

Don't ask long story. Any way I made a crack at us getting old knowing she wouldn't like it. Why people like to stay forever young? I always wanted to age. Still today I act older than the average person my age. And wish someday soon that all my facial hair turn gray. I'm known by the name Peace here at Valdosta. Nobody likes to be called by their birth right name in prison. The only youthful description is my entire upper body tattoos. Each drawing defines my personality and image. I guess it was both a fashion and personal statement to remind me. Who I am? My last expenditure was my girlfriend nickname Peaches tattooed on my left arm. Which I promise myself was my last. For that reason it bonded us closer. And a vital part of coping with this journey, someone who supports me. Although both social systems incurs the same trends. I received a letter from my girl the other day summarizing the events of her week. I played close attention to the part expressing such deep passion for the two most important people in her life. Mainly her way of securing her future. Also taking my advice. By editing such friends like Jude. Who don't deserve her company. It's inescapable meeting people who have a hidden agenda to hurt you. That's just like trying to breathe air while maintaining a proper heart rate.

... ...

When I wonder about my situation. Both good and bad things I'm learning to take inventory. Knowing my life has meaning and a purpose reflects who I am. Simply put living it becomes soothing to the soul. I have a world view that some people are separated from their core self. Meaning people who are unconvincing of their fake reality, and selfishness looking down on others. But I see them. As I see myself. Because at one point in my life I was too lost. Living without a purpose just to hurt others. Here in prison it's over populated with sub personalities among us. Groups who like to feel superior, better than the next man. Although those bullies take pleasure in that life. I never allowed it to dictate my direction. No matter what their motive was I felt just as tough. For instance someone yelled some very abusive words towards me from the top tier. This verbal abuse continued on for awhile, getting all the attention and applauding. But if I get on his level, foolishly. That means I would give this person control of me, taking way the peace. I need for myself as a security. Just think how foolish it would look. Again, if I was impatient not thinking this situation over. These reoccurring circumstances are easy to fall victim to. However the case you must be prepared to change the outcome for the better good.

So quite naturally. It was in my best interest to ignore him. Seeing our reality beyond our tiny imagination takes a determining will and effort. Not the description we rather choose. But it's in our favor. Your alter ego will never let you shine, so don't even listen to it. I'm talking about that real world. View we so unconsciously choose apart from our true nature. The bigger picture can only be captured by investing time to understand your natural process. Oppose to those conflicting issues that create problems in which prison itself can decide for you. Are you crazy?

When I finally got the courage telling my mama. Why I got expelled from school? She kind of knew already. What sheltering mother didn't know their child behavior? The teacher's may not have felt sympathy for me being mislead by others in my classroom. The class rooms were systematically ran similar to a case based operation. The kids that were A student's set in the front. While the failing students set in the back of the class. Normally my desk was in the back with the rousing trouble makers. Because Malcolm and I was sailing candy we stole from the store. He simply held the class attention including the teachers, long enough for me to make a dollar. But that didn't work in Ms. Brown's class room. She was like a bold eagle eyes on every thing. She missed nothing. And especially the kids in the back, she could spot trouble easy with her thick glasses. She just knew I was disrupting the class. Why I got blamed, trying to explain to the principal that it wasn't me. Such lessons came later on in my criminal career. That's when I realized. I'm better off doing things by myself, rather being punished for someone else mistakes also. I had to edit my friends in school after that, especially those times of doing wrong.

I had got tired of taking all the heat.

CHAPTER 32

As a result I'm content. And throughout the rest of this journey. It's hope I will continue following the spiritual to lead the way. It had definitely devised a plan for me. Prison is what it is. But it's up to me to keep focus beyond all the disparity intended to hold me here for an indefinite time. And let's be honest with ourselves. Brothers along with myself are in prison because we failed. Many of us never had a support system or opportunities that others had growing into our man hood. Any lack of basic needs such as stability, role model, safe outlet or purpose. Will eventually lead brothers down the wrong path towards a jail cell. Prison does not restore those conditions. It does not provide stability. It weakens. It creates violent behavior of destruction that takes away dignity. The world outside these walls remain blind to all the disparity that exist behind these walls. May we not forget the humanity of those we lock away. I write this story before you all. As a man of forgiveness who is no longer a criminal. I may not have the best reputation throughout my bid. But I'm well respected by staff and my peers behind these walls. In the time I've been on the Tier. My rapport was something rare, kept inside a cell, where movement was scarce. I'm only allowed recreation an hour a day. I'm escorted to the shower three times a week. It's a ugly sight.

But yet I'm still grateful for the smallest achievement of my life.

I'm a man with flaws, yes I'll admit some of my past behavior towards people was intentionally provocative. In a way to survive, the materialistic life I was hooked on. I thought I could have the best of what my society had offered. Man was I wrong. But in spite of all that instant gratification. There were times I set in my studio apartment, feeling something was definitely wrong. Like my life had no purpose.

Naturally men don't behave that way. They pursue life making choices based on their own individual views. They seek real values that gives them true happiness and contentment. Men just don't continue doing what didn't work, then expecting a different outcome. Fortunately for me, such experience of understanding became a resourceful solution to heal from a wounded past. However the results finally offered me much peace. Men are defined by their integrity. Measured upon goodness by giving to others. They do not settle for anything but rather use a discerning heart to distinguish between right and wrong. Men are generous and compassionate beyond being rich or poor. They give freely. How I hope men would act right? Just imagine, if America had a system set up for the rich to give 2.5% of their wealth to the poor annually. What if the GDC brought back the college courses offered to all state prisoner's? Or, what about a new prison reform, changing laws that over criminalize and punish offender's. It's not my call but my efforts towards making a change. By the same token. Meeting these conditions does not result in constant improvements. I have made some efforts trying to change the many problems in prison. It's not the self determination correcting the wrong. Because most of the time the resolution will be rejected, so is the effort worth it? Yes it is. That's just our misguided notion how things will turn out no matter how often we try. See what's important to remember is that the system was established to fail you.

Giving up. That is what occupies my mind giving up the fight. But the moral of the issue becomes my thoughts. Not understanding why the Warden or his guards are acting this way. I'm reminded that this system used a very effective process controlling humans. By simply dividing them up, using the differences among them. Such fear, distrust, and envy for control purposes. These methods of putting the offender in line is used today. That was established 300 years ago. If a person is trained to distrust all prisoners then how is it possible for them to behave fair towards them.

··· ··· ···

In the beginning. I talked about my childhood. As a young child raised by both parents along with a stable home. I was taught a basic education and such skills that later gave me better opportunities of becoming more independent. Inside the home choirs were shared fostering responsibility. And being taught the basic concept of living a pure life. I have a few examples, of how my family carried on the modern views of a African American family. I discovered many internal social problems which created a young prodigal child being influenced by others. From that transformation we learned about the different stages that brought about the change. How making unconscious decisions like rejecting my parents. Committing crime and dropping out of school changed my life. So, while in prison I began to struggle finding myself in the face of what seemed almost impossible. Making amends. That forged my spiritual growth. The power of the world. Welcomed it's way back into my life. How thoughts of chasing wealth for a meaningless cost only failed me.

As you inventory your life. Likewise, these events happen again and again over a period of time. We have been given a will making choices that are for the good or bad. In either case, the final outcome is not for us to make because the matter is beyond our control. Regardless what our circumstances are we do not have the power apart from God. To make it happen. How many times we've tried a different route only to end up with the same results? We spend months on lockup only to be released back into population. Then reenter three weeks later for violating another prison rule. Or better yet, we get released from prison after a probation violation. But a week later we commit a violent crime facing life in prison. Does this sound familiar to you? The flip side is leaving that life behind. You reflect back on the choices you've made relying on the direction your life is going. As you think aloud. I encourage you to let Devine intervention make you into the man God intended you to be. Let go and allow Him to reform your life. I guarantee you that life will have much more meaning than the former. You owe Him a dept. for all He has given you. A parent that labored and nourished you. Those guardians that took you inn providing shelter and food. Who knows you may change the game for the better.